Cockerel's in t... cut

Remembering a working boatman's life

John Blunn in the engine 'ole of *Cepheus*

Cockerel's in the Cut

Remembering a working boatman's life

by

John Blunn

Edited by Dr Lucy Waldron

and Peter Silvester

CANAL BOOK SHOP

Cockerel's in the Cut

Remembering a working boatman's life

by

John Blunn

Edited by Dr Lucy Waldron and Peter Silvester

Text and photographs © 2008-2016 John Blunn
Foreword © 2016 by Dr Lucy Waldron

First edition 2008 published by Delos Press, Birmingham

Second edition published 2016 by Canal Book Shop and reprinted September 2019
Audlem Mill Limited   The Wharf   Audlem   Cheshire   CW3 0DX
www.canalbookshop.co.uk   sales@canalbookshop.co.uk   01270 811059

ISBN 978-0-9955180-0-1

Dedicated to my late wife Mary,
my new wife Mavis,
and our children

Contents

Foreword to the second edition

Welcome to the second edition of this biography. It's been eight years since the first issue – which was a bit of a mission to get done, when you consider I live on the other side of the world for the majority of the time. It's been my privilege to know John Blunn all of my life. He and his wife, Mary, moved into the British Waterways Board house in the village of Wheaton Aston just weeks before I was born in 1970. They quickly became friends with my parents, Jack and Mavis Waldron, who lived at the nearby lock on the Shropshire Union Canal, first on a pair of old working boats (the josher *Daffodil* and converted butty *Cobham*) and later at the lockside. John and Mary played an important role in my formative years, as they had a daughter, Kathy, who was slightly older than me, and they would often take turns in babysitting duties with my parents. I can clearly remember evenings in Mrs Blunn's spotlessly clean house and immaculate garden - her pride and joy.

Of course the years go by, and, like a lot of 'boat kids', I denied my canal connections, which were the cause of much ridicule and bullying at school. I would never talk to my classmates about our family weekends away on canal 'digs' up and down the country, or my father's obsession with old engines and vehicles, mostly appeased by his work at the Black Country Living Museum in Dudley, where he and Mavis were volunteers and founder 'Friends'. Having other boating kids as friends made it easier to be 'different' compared to the housing-estate families we mixed with at school. As Kathy and I grew up, we rather lost touch, although I would still regularly see her parents, especially John, who worked our 'section' of canal.

As I grew older, I began to appreciate my boating childhood, and, of course, the love of canals never leaves you. I'd organise canal holidays with groups of friends, and became a volunteer caretaker and restorer of the Bolinder-powered Clayton's tarboat, *Stour*, for the Black Country Living Museum. Eventually I bought a 'proper' boat once more - a Star class 1930s little Woolwich unconverted motor, *Cepheus*, which I loved dearly.

When Mary Blunn died so sadly the year after my father, my mother and I attended the funeral in Penkridge. It was a proper boatman's do (which are becoming increasingly rare) with many of their extended family and old friends in attendance. Mary was greatly loved, and rightly so, as she was a super lady, and a good friend to all who knew her. At the graveside poor John looked terrible, and I felt we had to say something, so we invited him to come over and see our boat, and maybe take her out once in a while. A short while later, he did just that, and then kept coming back for more! Shortly after this, I emigrated to New Zealand, and was very grateful to John for his help in looking after the boat and helping with the moorings we still run at Wheaton Aston. Just before my divorce, *Cepheus* had to be sold, which was very sad. However I was not without a boat for long. Apart from borrowing various working boats, such as the lovely *Cactus*, owned by Malcolm Braine, and moving the South Midland boats from time to time, I really wanted my own again. I bought *The North*, a 1925 Midlands and Coast boat, in the summer of 2010, mainly as a residence whilst working in the UK, which is still her role for me to this day. She has come back into the family, as mum owned her in the 1960s, and she is a lovely boat. John bought half of her from me in 2012, as he and mum were using her more than I was! After much money and work lavished on her – she is very beautiful to handle and to live on.

We never dreamed that the original association with *Cepheus* would spark such a major change in John's life. Although things will never be the same without his beloved wife, both his daughter Kathy and I like to think that he and my mother have had great fun being out on *Cepheus* and, later, with *Stour* and *The North*. There is nothing so therapeutic as boating with old friends, especially at times when life is hard and it is difficult to see your way forward.

Whilst chatting with John on one trip, we encouraged him to write down his experiences of the canals, as his stories were so interesting, and he has a wealth of knowledge about the canal system. His family were very keen for him to do this too, and so he was persuaded to write this book, even though, as he points out, he has never attended school. Although I have helped with the editing, the work is essentially all his own. After many months of collating written notes and taped reminiscences, I felt it was important that the reader could `hear' John talking. It's been rather a nice change for me too, as most of the books I normally write are scientific texts, and not nearly so interesting!

There were plenty of others who helped in this process - and John and I would like to express our thanks to them, especially Dave Newell (*Stour*) for photos and Peter Silvester at Audlem Mill for publishing the second edition.

We can learn so much more about the canals and boats from people like John, who are happy to pass on their skills and knowledge to the next generation. It's always a joy to watch a born boatman steer a working boat round a tricky section. He has become quite the celebrity in his retirement - appearing on radio and television and in articles for newspapers and magazines. What a change from a 'quiet retirement'!

I trust you enjoy John's story, as well as the fabulous pictures spanning three generations of his family, which he has been kind enough to include. His life story is appealing not only to canal enthusiasts, but to anyone who has an interest in social history from the last century, and how it was to live and work on the boats - a way of life that has now all but vanished.

Happy reading.

Dr Lucy Waldron
July 2016

Chapter 1

Beginnings

My name is John Henry Blunn and I was born on the 16th of March 1934, in Albion Street, Wolverhampton, at my grandmother's house. My father, who I was named after, but was always called Jack, and mother was canal boat people, working for Fellows, Morton and Clayton. They had already got five daughters, and they had gone to live, temporary like, with me grandmother, ready for when mam gave birth to me.

John Henry Blunn, aged six months

A boy after having five girls! After about three years from when I was born, me mother had another girl, then later on she had another boy. That was the last, thank God. Mind you, most of us was from big families them days.

In the thirties, there was no work because of the Depression. My father went everywhere trying to find a job but couldn't get one, so in the end my parents went back to what they knew best, the canals. It was the only place there was any jobs, and as making a living on the boats meant that all the family went, that's how I come to be brought up 'on the cut' which is what boat families calls the canal.

My father could not afford to be out of work long, what with a wife and six kids to keep. There was no government benefits them days. If you didn't work you got no money, you didn't get fed or have anything for rent. Mind you, it meant that everybody pulled together, because nobody had much. I remember my mother and sisters walking miles to get some bread when the food was short. If she did get us some, we kids would eat it straight away without anything on it, you was that hungry.

Grandmother Blunn and John Blunn

Chapter 2

Boating Childhood

A lot happens when you are kids that you don't always remember, but if you've got older sisters they tell you things that went on when you were too young to realise. If it wasn't for family and friends around you, you would not have half the stories to tell! I have been fortunate to have older sisters that have told me things, but as you get older I have found that you do remember some major bits from when you was very small.

The canals was a hard life for my parents, having so many kids and both having to work the boats to earn a living. As was the way in them days, as their girls got older they used to help with the younger ones, so we was a very close family. Both my mother and father would work long hours, during daylight and after dark too, if they had to. The children would learn quick to help out with the horse and the locks, or helping with the younger children or getting meals ready. There's a lot of pride in keeping your boats and cabin clean and tidy. Not an easy task when you're working long hours with eight kids to look after!

The boat cabin, where we lived, was about eight foot by six, and we would all eat and sleep in here. Some boats would have a little cabin at the stem *(front end]* built into the bows where the children would sleep together. Mind you, most of the time we was all outside, on the towpath or the cabin top. In many ways it was probably a healthier life than many kids who lived in cities had, what with the fumes and dirt, disease and poor housing in them days.

My earliest memories are of horse boating, before we had a motor boat with an engine. The horse would pull the boat along using a rope that was attached to the mast, set about a third of the way back down the hold, where the cargo went. These boats hadn't changed much since canals first started, in the 1700s, as all there was were horses to move things around. In that way, over the years, boats had improved until they was pretty efficient, and the ways of doing things were all established.

When I were a lad, the locks still had all the little bits of metalwork and gaps in the foot bridges that you needed for handling all the lines, and the short wooden strapping posts that you could use to stop the boats by looping a strap round. These were to help you control the boat when you were using the locks. You can still see some of them, mainly the metal guards on the bridge holes, where the ropes would rub past, and the odd metal hook or 'split' foot bridge.

My parents worked two horse boats for Fellows, Morton and Clayton, and sometimes they had other men working with them, especially when us kids were too small to help out.

I was a bit of a handful as a child. When I was two years old, me and my older sister Doris was playing in the boat hatches by the back deck, and my mother was steering. Not being careful, I tippled over the side into the river at Nottingham. My sister shouts to my mother, 'The babby's in the river.' My mother looked round and seen me struggling in the water. She started to scream, and the man that was walking with the horse on the bank heard her. He ran back and jumped in the river and saved my life. He must have been a good swimmer, or I would have been a gonna. This man was named Billy Powell and he was working with my father and mother at the time. The shame of it is that I was never able to thank this man for saving my life, because one day he was walking down the towpath at Cheshire locks where there was an electric cable going across the towpath. It must have been live, because when he stepped on it, it killed him. It was a very sad thing to happen. I always remember that I owe my life to that man, God bless him.

When we was moored one time at the Port *(Ellesmere Port, Wirral)* my sister Doris was given some pears off a lady. Well, she wouldn't give me one, so after a few arguments she says to me, 'ere are then, you can have one.' Well, I had it off her, threw it at her and she falls and cuts her head open. Another time, in the cabin with my other sisters, they wouldn't let me do something or other, so I threatened to break the lamp glass and blame them!

I must have been a naughty boy back then, having a tantrum if I couldn't have me own way. Despite that, we were always very close growing up and have stayed that way even now.

Canals are dangerous places, and I had my fair share of scrapes, usually falling in! When I was about six years old, we was coming up the Staffs and Worcester Canal near Penkridge. My two older sisters, Eliza and Helen, was about a mile in front getting the locks ready for when the boats come to them, and they had me with them. But me being me, and into everything, when I was pulling the gate I slipped under the balance beam and into the empty lock by the bottom gate. I only went and picked one of the deepest locks *(Longford Lock* near Penkridge) on this canal, didn't I!

My sisters didn't know what to do, they couldn't swim, they hadn't got a pole or any rope, so they started to panic. But it seemed God was with us, for they seen a boat come round the corner, so they ran calling for help, for someone to bring a pole to get me out of the canal.

The man jumped off his boat with a short pole but when he got there he couldn't reach me, so he said to my sisters, 'Hang on to me legs and don't let go.' By leaning down far into the lock in this way he just managed to reach my coat, which was all that was keeping me afloat. My life was saved again. His wife gave me a horrible drink of salt water to make me sick, so that I would bring up the water that I had swallowed out of the canal - they always used to do that in them days. It must have done the trick, as I am still alive! The couple who saved me that time round was called Jack and Sarah Ready, and they was friends of my father and mother, or as close as you could get. You didn't have much time to keep up with many friends.

People on-the cut was always good to you when you needed a hand, though. When my father was took bad once at Wolverhampton, my mother worked helping other families down Wolverhampton locks to earn a bob or two. She would take one of us with her, and if the other family was better off than you, they would give you little things out of kindness. I was only very young at the time but I can remember this as if it was yesterday.

John Blunn

It's funny really, when my father and mother had all us children, my auntie Nelly used to do a bit of washing for us. She was full of life and jokes and her used to play tricks on my father. When she had done the washing for me mother she'd sew up shirt sleeves for my father and things like that for a joke. When my father tried to get them on, they wouldn't fit, and he would say, 'That Nelly has been here again, she's been playing one of her tricks.' The next time she saw him, her would say, 'That had you, eh Jack, that'll teach you.' And he used to say, 'You wait. I'll get you next time!' But they never held grudges, boat people.

Everyone would have a row sometimes. My mother used to row with various people. As kids, we'd meet up with other boat children and play together and then we'd fall out and hit one another, which would rile the adults. Mrs Nelly Jinks, especially, used to fall out with my mother about the kids, and whilst they were rowing we'd already made up and was playing again! Mind you, I'll say this for Nelly Jinks, when anyone was in trouble she was first on the scene. When my father died, she come up behind us on her boats. When she got to us, she went straight to me mother and gave her all the sympathy and help she could. It was like that-they'd be at one another's throats and the next minute they were the best of friends. In them days, what you couldn't do with your fists, you wouldn't do at all.

It was common for my father to walk with our regular horse from Wolverhampton to Manchester. He'd have a sandwich and a cup of tea off my mother at a bridge, and ate and drank walking along behind the horse. One foggy day, just past Nantwich about a mile, something frightened the horse and he jumped in the canal. My father couldn't hold him and he swam across to the other side of the canal where there was a wide hole and it was full of mud. The horse must have got stuck in there, and he drowned. My father couldn't see him with it being foggy, and he was calling to him, but he couldn't get out of the mud. My father was crying because he couldn't help the horse, and they found it dead in the wide hole. It broke my father's heart, because he loved that horse. He had another, but it was never the same.

As I got older, we had a pair with a motor boat. Sometimes we had one boat load going to one place and our other boat going somewhere else, so you would load your butty boat with the materials that went the shortest distance. Then the motor boat would carry on to the place furthest away that the second load had got to go. This kind of arrangement meant some of the children would stop with mother on the butty, and the rest would go with father on the motor boat. Us kids would love it when this happened - we used to call it 'going apart'.

Chapter 3

Wartime

My father and mother used to carry all kinds of materials, especially in the war years: copper, aluminium, steel tubes, army shells, army clothing, sugar, flour, tinned food, cheese, wheat, corned beef, timber, coal-everything that goes by road now. The canal was very busy with workboats in the 1940s. Sometimes my father would have what you call a 'flyload', which needed to be delivered very fast, so you had to work non-stop, night and day, until you got the load where it had to go.

When there was a lot of boats on the canal, this caused a bit of extra work at times, particularly when you met another horse boat coming towards you. If you was single-handed or didn't want the walk, then you could do what was called 'backering'. This was when you could let your horse go on its own at a fair rate, which would make things far easier, as you could ride on the boat. That was okay until you seen another horse boat coming, then you would jump off so you could pass the other horse safely. One of the drivers would stop his horse, then the other would hold the line up over the boat that you was meeting. Then you could get back on your boat if you was in between locks. Sometimes you would get a horse that would stop when you left it alone, so you would have to walk all the way with it from one end of the canal to the other.

There was tricks you could use if you couldn't backer the horse. You had to make believe there was someone walking behind him. To do that you'd tie a piece of rope with an old shoe on to the swindle stick *(the bar that goes behind the horse's tail)* so the horse would think there was someone behind him and he'd carry on. If you didn't do that, then when you got on the boat the horse would soon stop and look round as if to say, 'Well, he's got on the boat and I ain't walking all the way on my own.'

Working with horses could be a danger in itself. When we worked for Fellows, Morton and Clayton around Birnigum *(Birmingham)*, we would have a horse from Broad Street, Wolverhampton, to pull the butty boat up the locks. Boat horses was always given a name and a number - this horse was '44' and he was a bit wild. We was at lock no. 4 from the top, which was known to the boat people as Woods Lock, and it's at a very sharp bend by the railway bridge. I was standing by the corner, when a train came round and over the bridge.

The horse got frit *(took fright)*, took off and the line pinned me up by the steel corner of the bridge. The line was round my neck, and it could have taken my head off, but someone stopped the horse just in time.

If you tied up for the night with lots of other captains and boats, and you wanted to start off before them in the morning without them knowing, to get ahead and have a good road for the day, you'd tie hessian bags round the horse's feet. When you bought the horse out of the stable, they'd never hear you pass them, so you'd get off ahead of them. This wasn't so easy when we moved on to motor boats! If you wanted to get off afore them, especially a Bolinder, and how noisy they was, you used to get the pump what you used to pump the bilges, and you'd stick it down the exhaust pipe to silence the engine, until you got clear of them and they couldn't catch you. Boatmen was always up to tricks like that. Nothing dirty, but just as a matter of getting there first, the locks being ready for you, making it plain sailing.

You always hear a lot about how it were hard for boaters' kids to get to school. Some boat kids learnt to read and write on their own without going to school. Me and my brother and sisters did just that! We started by taking down boats' names and looking at comics like the Beano and the Dandy, and asking someone who could read to tell us what it meant. We would keep saying it and remembering the words and we just went on from there. As my wife, Mary, used to say, 'Never judge a book by its cover!' When you are learning by yourself you are not under any pressure, like the kids are at school now, with the teachers saying, 'come on, you can do better.' The little kids are so tired when they come out of school today. I see my grandchildren when I pick them up from school; their eyes tell it all. Because we were not under pressure and we wanted to do it ourselves, I think we learnt a lot better. We may not be 100%, but it was enough to get us through life.

As I got older, my father and mother stopped with the horses and got a motor boat. The first pair we had was a motor boat called *Panther* and a butty boat called *Fanny*. Well, my mother was not very happy with that name, as you can imagine! All the kids in the cities used to stand on the bridges and shout, 'Hello Missus, how's your Fanny!' My mother got so fed up with this, she got a cloth and hung it down over the boat's name! When the ticket office man used to take the boat's name down, they used to say to my mother, 'What's the boat called?' Without saying a word, my mother would pull the cloth up to show him the name then put it down again. She said to my father, 'Get another butty, I don't like the name of this one.' So he told the boss about it, and they gave him another one called *Coniston*, which the local kids didn't find nearly so funny.

When I was about eight years old I had my first pair of long trousers and that made me feel ten foot tall. We was loading flour at the time at Ellesmere Port. My mother said to me, 'Come into the cabin, I have got something for you.' When I seen them I was overjoyed! It was a big deal in them days. From that day on it seemed like I had grown up overnight, and when I seen my pals I would show off my new long trousers.

When we was tied up for a stoppage (*canal maintenance*), all the boys off the boats would go off all over the place. We didn't get into any trouble because if we did anything wrong, we would be in trouble with our parents, not like today, where kids don't worry about their parents or the law! We would go across fields and get run at by the bull sometimes, but we still used to get a bag of mushrooms.

It was funny where you'd get extra food and treats from sometimes. We was down Manchester docks, alongside a ship, loading, when someone emptied the ship's toilet out all over our boats! So my father went up on the ship and seen the captain. He made the crew come down and clean it up and apologise for the inconvenience. They couldn't do enough for us after that. They give us oranges and tinned food and everything! You know how it is when the captain's back's turned, the crew think they can get away with anything.

On one trip we was near Beeston near Nottingham, and we had a hell of a lot of rain. There was too much water about for us to travel the five miles on the river Trent, so we had to stop at Beeston. All the fields was flooded - it was like being at sea! All you could see floating down were the sheds out of people's gardens and dustbins and kennels, with the dogs on top of them sometimes! We don't know whether any of the poor dogs survived or not. We was pushed back by the flood to Nottingham Lock, and all you could see of the lock was the top of the paddles. We had to moor up against a factory on the off side, what used to store army clothes and stuff. That was the only way we could get off the boats to fetch anything from the shops - bread or milk. The fellows in the factory would give us bags of clothes and brass buttons, and they looked after us well. It was exciting for us kids, but not so good for our parents. We just had to wait there until the water went down.

A regular run for Fellows, Morton and Clayton was up to the Port for sugar. They'd load you up in the top level, where the museum is now. You'd go past the office and round the corner to where there was all warehouses in them days. The fellows would wheel out the bags of sugar, two hundred weight each, to the boat side, and the captains would grab it with both hands around at chest height and place it in the bottom of the boat, until they got so far along. The next lot would be placed cross-ways on the ones that was already piled up. It was hard work to lift two hundred weight of sugar. They'd load two boats like that.

If you were to load flour at the Port, you had to go down the two big locks, turn left, and round to a swing bridge, which was swung off while you went through to the flour mills. Flour bags wasn't so heavy as the bags of sugar, which were so hard to load. If you carried wheat, you'd take two loads of loose grain down to the Port and there was a big hopper with spoons on it going round and round, which would suck all the wheat into these scoops, take it all the way up to the top and empty it into the warehouse. When you got down to the last couple of tons you'd have to shovel it into the hoppers, as they couldn't suck it up no more.

If you'd got any broken boards in the bottom of the boat, the loose wheat would go down under them. Back at the depot you'd bag these stray bits of wheat up and give it to the lock houses where they had chickens, say, and they'd give you eggs or garden vegetables in return. Case of 'You scratch my back and I'll scratch yours'.

When we were kids we didn't have a lot of luxuries, but we did look forward to Christmastime. We would hang our stockings up, and our parents would put in what they could afford. It was normally an orange in the bottom, and an apple, perhaps a few nuts and dates, and maybe a Dinky toy or a new penny, if they had one. We used to look forward to emptying that stocking and was very grateful for what we got. Today people have too much and don't appreciate it, but you can't blame the kids for that. Mind you, I wouldn't want the life for the kids today, especially not my grandchildren.

The people in the warehouses that used to get you loaded put extra stuff on sometimes. They knew you hadn't got a lot of money, and, especially when the war was on, no-one had much food anyway. They'd never tell the captain they'd put extra on, mind. One day, we was in Manchester, at Castlefields, emptying two loads of tinned salmon. After my dad took the last load up to the warehouse, the foreman says to him, 'Have you had some of this salmon?' Well my dad says, 'No, we haven't.' 'Well, you should have done,' says the foreman, 'because there's five cases over.' They must have made a mistake at the other end. What we're going to do,' he says, 'is give you a case of this salmon and distribute the rest between ourselves.' So my father was over the moon, because it meant more food for us and me mum.

Outside occasions like this, my dad would never touch anything, except sugar. When you was loading sugar in the hessian bags, you'd take a special piece of wood that you'd use to scrape the hessian aside and the sugar would trickle out. You'd take a little bit from each bag, and scrape the hessian back over, so no-one knew you'd had any out of them. That was how you survived them days, and everybody knew that the boatmen had to do that, and everyone did do it. Sometimes when a captain off another boat was carrying, say, sardines or spam, and you were carrying sugar or grain, you'd swap one another. He'd give you a few tins of sardines and you'd give him a bit of sugar, and that's how it was. Nobody thought themselves thieves, it was just survival.

Mind you, the company always appreciated it when you was reliable in your work. We was at Wolverhampton, and my father went to the office to get the orders to see where he'd got to go and load, and the gaffer says, 'Jack, I want you down at Manchester for Monday morning, Manchester docks to load two full loads to Birnigum.'

This was a hard trip. We set off and got to the docks on time, loaded the two loads, and brought it straight up to Birnigum. The boss at Wolverhampton said to my father, 'Jack, when I give you that order, I knew I could rely on you, you done what I asked you and thank you very much.'

When the war was on, you might be at Birnigum or Manchester, and the sirens would go off. All the family would have to get off the boats and run to the nearest air raid shelter until the all clear went, then you could go back to your boats - that is if the cut had not been bombed. If that happened, then you could be homeless for a time, but there was usually some family that would take you in until you got some more boats sorted out from the company.

During the war, when we was anywhere big like Manchester or Preston Brook or Birnigum or Wolverhampton, the boatmen was sometimes called to do fire watch, and they had a special badge for this occasion. They'd be up all night walking about and seeing everything was alright. It was worrying because they all had families on the boats and they could get bombed any time, which did happen. A lot of times you had to go to air raid shelters when the sirens went. You could be there all night, and you never knew when you came back whether your boats was sunk, and some was in Birnigum. It was just pot luck really.

I remember once at Birnigum my father went up the slide hole *(the slide at the back of the cabin)* of the boat and he got hit with a piece of shrapnel, from part of a bomb, and it cut his head open. It was very worrying them days, because you didn't know if you was going to be bombed or not.

After a shelling raid, the Germans would discharge their shell cases on the way home, which would land anywhere, just about all over the place; on the bank, in the canal, up the woods. You'd be going along and you'd see quite a few of these big brass shells lying about. When they dredged the canals, loads of them would come up in the mud. People would get them out and wash them off and use them. The biggest ones would make nice brass chimneys, you'd just cut them off so they fit properly.

When we was on rations, and you had your ration books and clothing coupons, you had what you could, and then had to wait until you was entitled to some more. Mam and dad would maybe have two eggs, which they'd boil, and cut off the tops and us kids would have these on toast, whilst they ate the rest of the eggs. These things makes you appreciate not to waste what you have.

John Blunn on Samuel Barlow's motor boat *Tiger* at Cosgrove Lock,
Grand Union Canal, 1958

Chapter 4

Carrying for Clayton's

After a while, my family gave up working for Fellows, Morton and Clayton, and went to work to another company, Thomas Clayton of Oldbury. One of the bosses there, Jack Craddock, knew my father quite well, and he asked him to come and work for them.

The change to another company's boats meant they would be carrying black oil from Ellesmere Port, at Stanlow on the Manchester Ship Canal, to Langley Green, near Oldbury in the Black Country. We got another pair of boats, the motor they had was named *Umea* and the butty boat *Pinn*.

Umea was fitted with a Bolinder engine, a single cylinder semi-diesel engine designed in Sweden early in the 1900s. Bolinders are started by putting your foot on a spring-loaded pin that comes out of the flywheel. You have to swing your weight over the top to make the flywheel move. When the engine fires, it throws the flywheel back in the opposite direction to the way it's kicked over, and sometimes the engine starts up in reverse. My father had an accident kicking this Bolinder off, when it kicked back *(fired whilst he was kicking it over)* and broke my dad's leg. He never seemed to get over that injury, and it started him worrying about his family a great deal.

One day, not long after, we had a message to say my sister Mary had lost her only child at Ellesmere Port. My father had just had a bit of compensation for breaking his leg, and, as my sister and her husband were quite poor at that time, my father gave her this to bury the baby.

I was still good at falling in the cut, when I was old enough to know better! We was at Audlem, just reached the Bottom Lock. My two sisters put the bottom paddles up to empty the lock. I went to walk over the bottom gate and into the canal I went, with the two full paddles up, fortunately not on the lock side of the gates. The water washed me down the canal into the bridge, and my dad just managed to catch me as I was going under for the last time.

I once fell in at Oldbury, in all that dirty water. After that I learnt to swim - and not before time neither! I still used to fall in the canal, but it meant I didn't have to wait around for someone to pull me out.

Ben Smith and John Henry 'Jack' Blunn at Bunbury in 1948

Other people weren't so lucky when it came to being in the canal. When my wife was a young girl working with her grandfather on the Clayton's horse boats, they were coming up the Port pound, between Ellesmere and Chester. Mary saw what she thought was a doll in the canal. She says, 'Get the boat hook for that doll, Grandad,' and when he looks, he sees it isn't a doll, it's a tiny baby. Anyway he had to report it to the police when he got to Chester - he told the lock keeper, who went to the local station for him and gave them the details. They got the baby out, and when their boat got to Oldbury, they sent the local police round to interview Mary. They asked her what did she think when she saw this baby in the canal - as she said she thought it was a doll, and told them how she'd asked her granddad to fetch it out for her.

It wasn't an uncommon thing to see bodies floating about in the cut. When I was a young lad, my mam and dad was near Brewood, and they come across this man in the canal, drowned. He had ginger hair, and my parents knew him from the pub in Brewood. My dad shouted to my mum, 'Stop in the cabin, you can't see this.' Dad reported it to the police, and they got him out and investigated it. I don't know if he threw hisself in or fell in by accident when he was a bit drunk, but my dad had to give evidence at the inquest about how he'd found him.

The most important in life is doing the things that are right and doing them well. When I was young, I was in charge of a horse and boat and I had to learn how to look after the horse and how it reacted. Mostly I had to feed it and clean it and see it was kept safe when we was travelling. Sometimes, if a horse had a bad shoulder, it would always pull towards the canal and so you had to tie the reins so it would stay into the bank. Then when you had time you'd have a look at its shoulder and see if it were inflamed or had broke out, then you'd have to get some stuff from the ostler *(professional horseman who took the place of a vet)* to rub on to make it heal. Then you'd have to have his collar pulled in to stop it rubbing on certain spots, and you did this because your horse was the main thing. Without the horse we couldn't get a living.

Talking about the harness, in the morning you'd go to the stable, very early, and you'd 'gear' the horse and put the collar on first and then the omes *(steel bars which go round the horse's neck and to which the harness is hooked)* and the gears and the bridle. Then you'd make sure they was on safe, and you made sure by pulling the belly strap up tight to keep the gears on. Then there was what you'd call a stirrup that would go under his tail, tied nice and tight and neat. Along from the bobbins on the harness there was a piece of wood going across just behind his legs with a hook on, called a swindle tree, or a v-shaped rope called a spreader, and you fastened the line to this to pull the boat. With a spreader you had to make sure it was put up onto the harness on a peg so it wouldn't drag behind his feet. There was lots to take into consideration when gearing a horse, but you just learned mostly as you went along.

On the Walsall Canal, 1951

Sometimes the horse would get frightened by a train or someone blowing a horn and if he jumped he might go in the canal. It was your responsibility to guide him to the shallowest place and get him back out again. It wasn't always easy on the BCN *(Birmingham Canal Navigations)* as there was some very deep spots, but you would find somewhere to get him out. Sometimes he'd wind himself by falling.

I had a tricky horse once. She was ok if you didn't drive her, when she'd got the nose tin on *(see photo above for a nose tin)*, when she were feeding, but she was very nasty if you treated her bad. I remember she once kicked a fella and broke his arm. She had a habit to kick out sometimes. I used to give her the odd lump of sugar, and sometimes when I'd whistle she'd come back to me. Like a human, you befriend a horse and it'll look after you.

You would always keep your horses looking nice. You would paint the bobbins on the harnesses red, white and blue, or you paint them twisted and you would black the leather harnesses and polish the brass. Sometimes, you would plait the horse's tail to make it look nice, and on the 1st of May you always dressed the horses up with crochet covers on their ears. If you looked after a horse and gave it a sugar lump now and again, you could whistle him and he would come to you because he would remember that lump of sugar. I used to have a mare called Bet. I trained her well and could whistle her up no problem, but if you hit her she would kick your brains out, so you didn't have to hit her, only talk to her. Horses are like human beings, if you treat them right they will do the same.

John Blunn and Bet in 1951

Chapter 5

Iced-up

In early 1947, we was frozen up for a long time at Wolverhampton. All the men on the boats had to go on the ice breaker, to break up the ice all round the BCN. The ice was that thick it used to stop the ice boat, even when they had about ten horses on the boat and there were about twelve men on the boat rocking, and all them others on the bank with the horses. At night, the boat captains used to make a hole in the ice and rake the coal out the middle of the cut for their stoves. There was lots of coal in the canal them days, as there was a lot of joey boats (*day boats, often with no cabin*) going round and there was always spilled coal. Knowing these things was how you and your family survived.

We haven't had a winter like that since. The ice was that thick it was unbelievable. It must have been very hard on our parents to make a living. Sometimes you'd get frozen up in the middle of nowhere and you'd have to walk miles and miles just to get your food. We were froze up one year between Audlem and Hack Green, and my father and my two older sisters walked to Nantwich to get bread and milk, and was away hours, as it were a long walk. My sister Mary was going to get married to Tom Powell at Nantwich, but as we got stuck for a long time, they had to make arrangements to get married at Wolverhampton instead.

My two other sisters, Eliza and Helen, got married at Nantwich - a lot of boat people got married there. You could not afford a big wedding, so you got married where there was a small community. Today, people have very big weddings at a very high cost and most of them don't seem to last together for long.

Tom Powell had a single Josher (*a boat built for Fellows, Morton and Clayton, named after its director Joshua Fellows*), *Tench*, and I'd go with him to make a cup of tea and be a help, watching the tiller whilst he done various jobs. It was common for kids to be 'borrowed' between boaters, 'specially if you was low on crew. We went to Wigan once with a load of sauce, and when we'd emptied that we come back and picked a load up at Preston Brook. The same when my sister Helen was courting Albert Clowes, I went with him as a mate, with his Clayton's horse boat. I weren't that big, so I couldn't work the horse, but I could steer whilst he did the horse. When they got married, I went back to my

John Blunn's sister Mary with husband Tom Powell and baby daughter Violet, and his brother Bill

parents' boat. Being away from the family and helping others meant you learned a lot about work and responsibility early on, which made for good lessons when you had to take on your own boats.

Later in that year a very sad thing happened. We was coming to the bottom of Audlem Locks and my father said he didn't feel very well, so my mother told him to go up to the doctor's in the village. She said, 'Me and the kids will bring the boats up to the Town Lock and meet your there,'- that was four locks up from the bottom. We got up there and moored up, but my dad had not come back. So my mother said to me, 'Go and see if you can see your dad coming.' I went down the road and I could see a crowd of people. I sort of pushed my way through, and there was my dad lying in the road. I shouted 'Dad!' and a policeman came over and said to me, 'Come on, son, take me to your mother.' I run in front of the policeman, but when I got back to the boat I didn't speak a word. Everybody was so upset, because my father had dropped dead before he got to the doctor. My mother told us later, she said, 'When I seen John's face, I knew something bad had happened.'

My mother was left with a pair of boats, me and two sisters, and our younger brother. I was only about 13 years old. Three of my elder sisters were married and had boats of their own, and I had another that was living with a family in Middlewich, working in a factory there. My sister Helen and her husband, Albert Clowes, said they would have my two sisters with them. They also worked for Thomas Clayton's of Oldbury, running to Ellesmere Port, so Doris and Irene went with them till they got married. My sister, Mary, and her husband, Tom, they come and worked our motor boat, and me and my mother and younger brother had the butty boat. We worked them as a pair in this way for about three years.

During this time, when I was about sixteen I remember we would have a horse from Cut End *(Autherley Junction).* The horse was to pull the butty boat up Wolverhampton Locks, and then it had to be taken back to Cut End. One of us would take the horse back, and then catch two buses and meet the boats at Tipton. Then you could get your dinner before you got to Oldbury.

One day, we had been to Windsor Street and loaded a lot of tar oil to take to Oldbury and we was travelling along below Smethwick locks and we hit something in the bottom of the canal. The boat nearly capsized, but it righted itself in the finish and my mother squealed and said, 'We've hit something and there's oil coming out behind the boat, a stream of oil.' So we had to drive as fast as we could to Oldbury and when we got here we had to take priority in the tar works and take all the oil out before the water started coming in.

We'd knocked the bottom up, and so we had to go on the dock and they had to fix it for us. These are things that happen boating, and still happens now. You don't know what's in the bottom of the canal, and when you've got a load of tar, then fortunately the heavier oil comes out first before the water can get it. So you're safe whilst the oil is coming out, but when it stops, you're going to sink. It's a matter of how far you are from the depot before you can unload; otherwise you've got a sunken boat on your hands.

John Blunn's Samuel Barlow pair, *Tiger* and *Warwick*, waiting to load at Atherstone, 1958

Chapter 6

A Young Boat Captain

In about 1950, me and my mother and young brother had a horse boat working local around the Midlands. Because Thomas Clayton's would not have a woman as captain, I had to be captain of a horse and boat, and I was only 17 years old, but we managed.

We were going down the 11 locks once and met a boat. As he went into the lock above he must have put a paddle up and when the gate went bang, the back water sent our boat into the lock at such a force my mother had to put the rope round the gate to stop the boat from hitting the bottom gate, but as she whipped it round the stud she got her finger caught in the rope and it cut half her finger off. She had to be rushed in to hospital. That upset everyone.

Working on the canals is so dangerous because you have to be very quick at your job. It is like driving a car. If you don't stop in time, you run into danger. With a boat you haven't got any brakes, 'specially not on a butty boat! Like I say about danger, we would set off from Oldbury very early every morning. When I got to the bridge above top of Smethwick, I would jump off with the bike and go and fill all the locks before the horse and boat got there, and you would do the same at Farmer's Bridge Locks. It was always black dark, that was the main danger, but you didn't look at it that way.

I remember what happened to a family that was working up Wheaton Aston Lock (*on the Shropshire Union Canal*) in the dark. Their 13 year old son fell into the lock and went down the paddle gear and drowned. He was a lovely lad too. Tragedies like this happened to lots of other families too, no matter if they'd been boating all your life. Thinking of all the times I fell into the canal, I must have been one of the lucky ones, for there was always someone to pull me out!

I remember once, we'd just emptied at Majors, on the north side of Wolverhampton, and we was going back into Oldbury. Going through Bilston and Hickmanses, a train went over the bridge and it frightened the horse, and she galloped off, dragging the boat with her. There was sparks flying from her hooves right up at the edge of the canal. My mam was shouting to me, 'Get away from her – she'll kill yer.' I was hanging onto her to keep her away from the canal and I managed to stop her eventually, but it was touch and go, I can tell you.

When I was nineteen I had to go in the army. This meant my mother and younger brother was not getting a living, because my brother was not old enough to be in charge of a horse and boat. To get round this, my mother went everywhere to try and get me out of the army. She did win in the end, but that took eight weeks. All this time, I was doing my army training at Wrexham in Cheshire *(actually, in Denbighshire)*. I used to come home on leave some weekends but I had to go back on Sunday afternoon for training on Monday. Then one day they called my name, 'Private Blunn, no.22858929, D company, Section 6, to report to the Head Officer.' I was thinking 'What have I done wrong?' When I got in the office they told me I was going home tomorrow. They said, 'Under the special circumstances we are discharging you, but if a war should break out we would call you back because you have been trained.' So I went home and I was in charge of a horse and boat again.

We used to start off very early in the morning. My mother would call me up about 2 am.

I used to sleep in the fore-cabin and if I didn't get up she would come and call me again. I would get up and go and gear the horse, and by this time my mother would have the boat ready. I would peg the line to the horse and off we would go. When we got to the Anchor Bridge *(Oldbury)*, I would get on the boat and have a cup of tea and a piece of cake. Until the Turnover Bridge you would have to stop with the horse most of the way if you wanted to stay in front of the other boats. There was no way they would pass once you got to the top of Farmer's Bridge Locks. It would be black dark all the way down Farmer's Bridge Locks; you had to work hard for your money in them days.

When we worked a pair of boats on the Shropshire Union Canal, up the flights of locks you had to use a long line that would reach from one lock to the next lock so that the motor boat would be in one lock and the butty boat would be in the lock below. So that when the motor boat went out of

Sammy Walters and John Blunn at Oldbury, 1950

34

the lock it would pull the butty boat out of the lock below. You would always have someone to empty the lock so as the motor boat went out of the lock, it was empty for when the butty boat got there. You set ahead like that at every lock until you got to the top lock, then you would wrap the line up until you got to the next flight of locks.

You only used this way of towing when you was going up the locks loaded. When you was empty you would bowhaul the butty boat down the flight. This was done by pulling the boat with a short line like you would use when a horse was pulling a boat. Mind you, the horse would have all the harness on to pull the boat as straight as possible. But when you was pulling it, if there was a few of you to pull the boat you could just get the line around your shoulders and pull together. If you was on your own, you would make a strap harness that fitted over your shoulders so that you was pulling with your shoulders and your hands was free, like the horse. You would do that at every set of locks you got to, and when you had pulled a boat down flights of locks like Wolverhampton 21 or Audlem, you had done enough! But that was your job, so you got on with it.

You had to be organised if you wanted to get through the day being fed and keeping up to date with all the jobs around the boats. We always kept our boats clean, and then there was the washing to be done, and baking and getting the food ready for eating, timing it for when you were travelling between locks. You would make sure the engine room and the Bolinder was always clean.

There was always something to do on a boat, like keeping the top tank full up and greasing the engine, and filling the lubricators up, or packing the spindle or changing the jet. Then there's other jobs, like putting a cylinder head joint on, cleaning out the mud box (*where the silt from the Bolinder water intake is deposited*) and the silencer and exhaust pipe, and packing the stern gland sometimes when it starts to drip.

Keeping body and soul together meant getting the shopping, carrying cans of water. Scrubbing the decks and rope work, cleaning the brass and splicing the rope were just a matter of pride in your boats. We also made rope fenders and a mop for each boat. Yes, there was plenty to do, but boat people could turn their hands to anything. That was because you didn't have anyone to tell you what to do, how to do it, so you made your own minds up and tried doing things as an experiment. If it didn't turn out right first go, you did it again until you did get it right. You know the old saying, 'If at first you don't succeed, try, try again' and that's what we would do. The world would be a better place if people were given more time to do their job and think for themselves then they would do a better job. I know because I always tried to do a good job because I didn't let people rush me. I used to say, 'If a job is worth doing it's worth doing right.'

Boat people would often get attached to horses, or boats or engines. With the Bolinder you would put your hand on her belly whilst the lamp was on, the cylinder as it were, and say,

'Come on old girl, don't let me down,' and sometimes it would work, she would start with the first kick. But if she let you down, you would swear at her – it didn't do any good, but you would do it all the same! The reward you got from a Bolinder was when you was travelling at night, when the engine would sing to you in the night air. You could also sing yourself, at the top of your voice with nobody to tell you be quiet!

When I was working at Oldbury, a little boy went missing, the local policeman's son. As we knew the canals like the back of our hands, they asked me and another boatman, Joe Shaw, to help them drag the canal. Fortunately they found him safe on his bike at Wednesbury. His father, Mr. Fishwick, biked all the way from Oldbury to Wednesbury to give us a nice letter to thank us for our help and experience with the canals. I wish I hadn't lost that letter over the years.

Working days could be very long; you'd start and finish in darkness. One morning, we started early from Oldbury. We was going to Polesworth to fetch a new dock boat back, so it was dark all the way down Smethwick, Farmer's Bridge and the 11 Aston Locks. Working locks in the dark is dangerous, and lots of people have been injured or died doing it, so you have to watch your step. It didn't get daylight until halfway down Minworth. I wouldn't do it again, but them days I was young and it was your living.

Some days you got back into Oldbury and you would think you had finished, but Caggy Stevens would ask you to fetch a rubbish boat back for him. You would take a loaded boat down to Moxley on the Walsall Canal and bring an empty one back just for a pound - about six hours work! Me and Joe Chatin would do that two or three times a week, and the empty boat was always half full of water, so we used to have to pump it out before we could bring it back.

At that time, me and two more lads off the boats were pals, we used to go everywhere together. Some of the time we would bike from Oldbury to Wheaton Aston, put up a tent and stay the night. Most of the time our bikes didn't have any brakes, so we used to stop them by putting the heel of our shoe on the back tyre of the bike. You didn't half wear some shoes out! I remember one time my handlebars broke, but that didn't stop us. We put in a steel bar where the handle bars should be and off we went again. We used to have a wind up gramophone to put records on and we had a radio that was powered by an 'accumulator', a glass bottle that had acid inside it that you had charged up at a garage like a battery.

We also used to swim in the canal regular, and if you couldn't swim you got a car inner tube, blowed it up and put it round your body under your arms and it used to keep you afloat until you learnt to swim.

Chapter 7

Courting Mary Nixon

There was family called Nixon that worked for Thomas Clayton who used to have two horse boats running from Oldbury to Ellesmere Port. They could not go down the river with their horses, so there was a packet tug that used to take them down to Stanlow. When they was loaded, it would bring them back to the river lock. From there they could use their horses again, and head for Langley Green in the Black Country. Well, they had three daughters, and I fell in love with one of them. Her name was Mary Margaret Nixon and she was a beautiful and very hard working girl.

Mary used to look after her grandmother and work the boat with her granddad. She was only fifteen then but she had been doing that since she was about 11 years old. We only used to see each other one night a week, what with me working around Oldbury and them going all the way to Ellesmere Port. But if they were going from Oldbury on the Saturday morning, what with me not working weekends, I would go with them down the Shropshire Union Canal, stay with them on the Saturday night, then go with them to the bottom lock of Adderley on the Sunday afternoon and then bike all the way back to Oldbury up the towpath. Most of it was uphill and most times it was dark before I got back to Oldbury. I had to bike home about 45 miles, but that was the price of true love!

Later on, they had to go and work from Leamington Spa to Banbury. That meant we could not see each other very often, because I was still working around Oldbury. So on a weekend, if they was going to be near Leamington Spa or Banbury, I would get a train and go and look for them. Sometimes I would walk miles until I got to them. I always used to find them in the end, but I would have to go back Sunday to go to work on Monday morning. Although it was a hard life, it was a good one in many ways, as you didn't get time to get bored!

We would go to the pictures if we could get some money from our mam or dad. If you asked a girl if she was going to the pictures and she said yes, you would say, 'Alright I will see you inside,' because you didn't have the money to pay for her! They would tell you where they would be sitting, and they would save you a seat by them and when the lights came on you would go and sit by them and hold hands. When you came out, you would buy them some chips.

When I started courting Mary Nixon, I asked her if I could take her to the pictures, as you did, and she said yes. I got my little brother, Bill, to go to her boat to see if she was ready to go. She was and we walked up the Clayton's yard to go to the pictures together. We was both so shy! But we got over it and was courting five years before we got married.

Later, Thomas Clayton gave her family a motorboat and had the horses off them, so that meant Mary had to learn all about the Bolinder engine. Her granddad was getting on, so he couldn't kick the engine off, which left Mary to do it all. My brother-in-law learned Mary a lot about Bolinders, and, of course, I used to help her when I could. This change meant they was running to Ellesmere Port again. This time they had to go down the river under their own power to load on the Ship Canal. It was not very nice when you used to meet the big ships, 'specially if you got too close to them.

They did that until the Ellesmere Port run gave up, so that meant most of the families had to go and work for other companies. Some went to British Waterways, but my girlfriend's family went to work for Samuel Barlow's Coal Carrying Company. They

Jane Nixon and her Thomas Clayton horse boats, with daughters June and Mary, being towed up the Manchester Ship Canal from Shell-Mex, Ellesmere Port, 1949

38

gave them a motor boat named the *Daphne*, which had a Petter engine in it. Mary had to get used to that as well.

They also had two butty boats, the *Matilda* and the *Little Marvel*, running down the Ashby Canal to load coal from Measham to the power station at Tusses Bridge. They did two trips a week because the run was pretty quick, as there was only one stop lock and the lock at Sutton Stop *(the boaters' name for Hawkesbury Junction, near Coventry, where the Oxford Canal meets the Coventry Canal)*. This meant I could see Mary more, often most weekends.

Work was getting short at Clayton's, so my mother and brother went to live with my sister Violet and her husband at Middlewich. I stayed at Clayton's, but I could not work a horse and boat on my own, so they give me a motor boat. I had the run to the gas works in Wolverhampton Locks. To make the trip, you had to turn around at lock No. 9 and go backwards down five locks, because you could not turn around in the gas works pound, and you had to be facing towards Wolverhampton to go back up the locks to Oldbury! I did that every day, for five days a week, every week.

Moving to Barlow's

In 1955, I went over to see Mary, and we had a talk and together we decided that I would give up my job with Thomas Clayton's and go and work for Samuel Barlow's. So I went and seen them, and they was delighted we had made this decision. They made arrangements to send a man and a van to come to Oldbury and pick up me and my things, and take me to Shackerstone where Mary and her family were froze up. So I had the spare butty boat until we could get to Sutton Stop. When the ice cleared we was able to move our boats, and when we got to Sutton Stop there was a van coming to pick me up and take me to Braunston to pick up the *Beatty*, a steel motor boat to go with the spare butty boat as a pair.

Now that I worked for Samuel Barlow's, it meant that me and Mary could see each other every day, but she still had her work to do as I had mine. One day Mary

Mary at Brewood Bridge, Shropshire Union Canal, 1953

was took very bad, so we had to send for a doctor at Stoke Golding. We didn't know what it was, but he gave her a needle and some tablets and after a few days she was much better. It was very worrying at the time, but you always worry when you love someone. She got better and she was at it again, always working and cleaning. She was a very clean young woman and she was like that all through her life; she couldn't stand filth.

Mary's grandfather Steve Dulson, on Thomas Clayton butty *Oka*

I now had a pair, and I took Mary's sister with me to work the one pair, and Mary worked the other pair with her mother and granddad until we decided to get married. We worked like that for about eighteen months, then, on the 17th of December 1956, we got married at Shackerstone, on the Ashby canal. When we got married, Barlow's was very good to us and gave us a sum of money as a wedding gift and wished us all the very best. The next day we had to go to Measham to load our boats with coal and take it to Coventry power station at Tusses Bridge.

Then we got married and we was very happy together. After the time that Mary had in her young life, I was like a guardian angel sent to be with her at all times and I was always with her. This didn't mean I made all the decisions - Mary made most of them and I used to go along with it, because usually when she made her mind up, it turned out right.

Mary was a very clever woman. Yes, we used to have our disagreements but every man and wife disagree on something or other, but it's saying you are sorry to one another that's most important in married life, because life's too short to disagree all the time. If you can have a good laugh together, it means a lot and I will say that me and Mary used to have a good laugh very often.

On the two Thomas Clayton boats to the left (butty *Oka* and motor *Severn*) are
Rose Nixon, June Nixon, Steve Dulson and Mary Nixon - Chester, 1954

Boating was a hard life, but a good one. You'd have to work in hail, rain or sunshine, but that was the way I was brought up - that was your living. So you just got on with it. There was many a time you got wet through -so you'd just change your clothes, wherever you could - in a lock or under a handy bridge. You have a hot drink and carry on because you had to get the order delivered.

After a while, Barlow's bosses asked us to work on the long runs down the Grand Union Canal to London and that area. We couldn't refuse them, because they had been very good to us, so from then on we was doing the long runs. We had to change boats, and we ended up with the motor boat *Ann* and the butty boat *Irene*, an ex-Harvey Taylor butty. But this butty was a very big Northwich butty, so we had another one named *Warwick*, a very nice boat. We had our eye on a better pair of boats we'd seen, so we asked Barlow's if we could have them. They didn't refuse so we ended up with two very nice boats, the motor *Tiger* and the butty *Gertrude*, and we had this pair until we finished boating. We could have had the *Raymond* new. Barlow's asked me to have this boat, but I said, 'Let an older hand have it,' as I didn't want to get any bad blood between us and the older captains, so they gave it to Arthur Bray. From then on, we was always good friends with the Brays, the Whitlocks, the Collins and the Peaslands and many more.

This was a busy couple of years for us. We used to get back from London, after doing the Jam 'ole (*Kearley & Tonge's jam factory at Southall*) or Nash Cocoa, or Croxley or Kings Langley, or Ovaltines or Home Park and travel back to Braunston to refuel and get your money, and anything we needed, like ropes. Then we would go to Sutton Stop and go to the office to get our orders and find out where we had to go to load. It might be Pooley Hall, Baddesley, Griff or Bedworth or even Longford. The closer you got to load near Coventry, the quicker you would get to London, but if you had to go to places like Pooley Hall or Baddesley it would mean two extra days before you would leave Coventry. If you had to go to Baddesley, there may be two or three pairs of boats to load in front of you, so the day would be gone before you got loaded. Then you had to clean your boats before you could set off.

John and Mary at Shackerstone on their wedding day, 17 December 1956

It was even longer if you had to go to Pooley Hall, because you had to go all the way down Atherstone, then you had to travel a few miles before you got there, and then you had to travel all that way to go back. The boats that loaded at Longford or Bedworth would be half way to London by the time you got to Sutton Stop! We used to have many a row with the man in the office at Sutton Stop, Mr Shaw was his name. He would send you all the way to Pooley Hall or Baddesley, and there would be only you and your wife to go all the way to Atherstone and back, and then he would give another captain, with about five or six in the family, a short loading place like Longford or Bedworth, when it should have been the other way round!

For them that had extra in the family to help up and down the locks, long loading points was not so hard, but you just could not make him see that. By going the farthest to load, this meant you had to work longer days to get your trip done in a week, but we did manage it somehow. I remember if me and Mary was working in the rain up locks and we got wet through, we went to change while the last lock was filling, and off we would go again. If we

John and Mary in the cabin of *Warwick* at Braunston, 1957

was working in steady rain all day, we would only change once; if we got wet again we stayed that way till we moored up at night.

We was coming up the pound between Fenny Stratford and Cosgrove. We was travelling empty and Mary was in the butty cabin, which was on cross straps up close to the motor. This gave her chance to see to the baby whilst we was going along. Well the wind blew me on the side and I just couldn't get off. I shouted to Mary for come give me a hand, but she never came out, whether she heard me or not I don't know. I lost my temper and threw the shaft in the canal. At that moment Mary come out of the butty cabin and says to me, 'You silly twit, you've thrown the shaft in the canal and you've got to get it out before you can get the boat off.' She came on the motor to operate the engine while I shafted the front end off. We had a good laugh about it after.

We was running to Measham, and Mary had these couple of bantam hens and a cockerel, who was a terror. Once he got out of the cage you could not catch it – I've chased him miles cussing him. We got to Snarestone tunnel, and the cockerel was out, and he flew up on the gunwhale of the boat, and went into the canal in the tunnel. Mary shouted to me, 'That cockerel's in the cut,' and I had just painted my chimney on the motorboat and it wasn't dry, so with all the commotion I had to stop, the chimney caught the top of the tunnel and knocked it in the canal. I wasn't very happy about that and I said, 'I'll kill that cockerel when I get it out,' and I had to get the mop and get the bird on the mop to swing it into the bottom

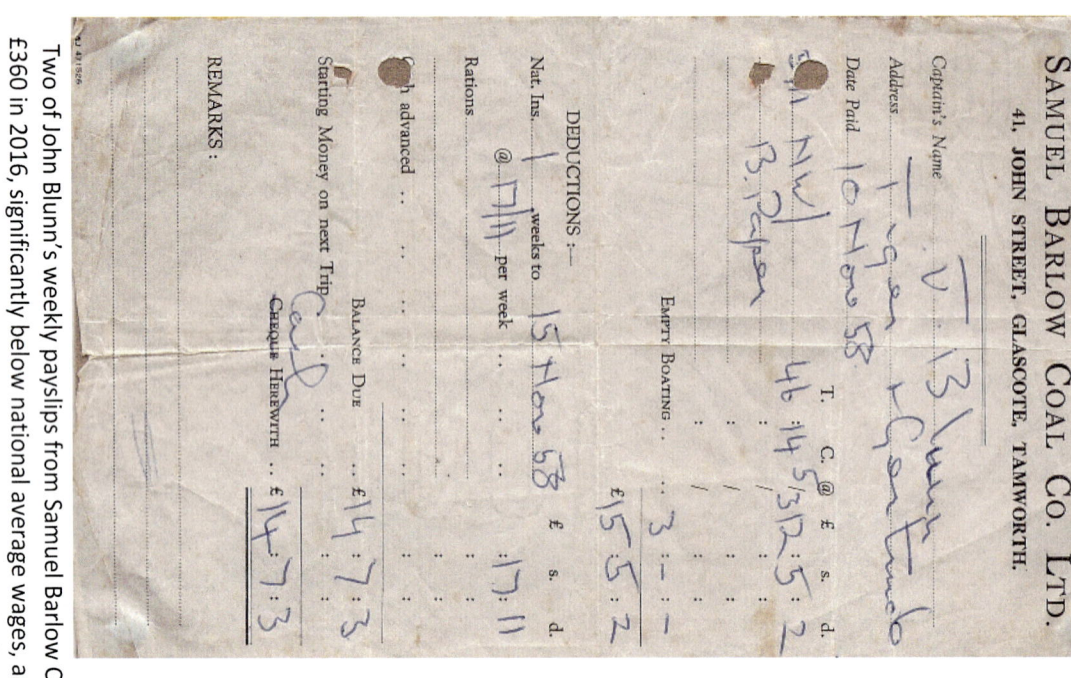

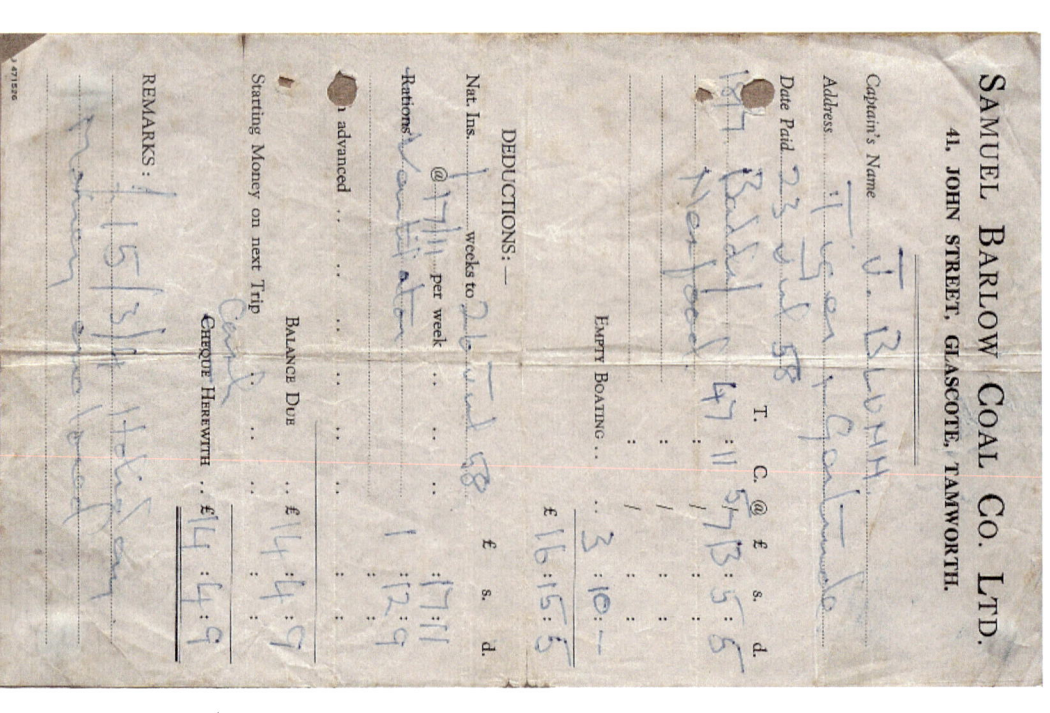

Two of John Blunn's weekly payslips from Samuel Barlow Coal Co. Ltd. in 1958. The gross pay equates to about £330 to £360 in 2016, significantly below national average wages, and about £150 below the average for modern day equivalent, lorry drivers, who no doubt work significantly fewer hours.

Ann and *Irene* at Sutton Stop, 1957

of the boat. I'll tell, you we laughed about that later too. The two little hens would lay every day, and we'd have an egg each. But one day at Sutton Stop, a stoat or something got at them and bit one of their heads off. Mary was very upset about that.

I remember one fellow and his wife, Sam Beech his name was, he was a real darling; he used to make Mary laugh with the way he'd tell jokes. We'd meet him and he'd say 'Have you got a fag? Give the missus a couple of fags and I'll give you them back when I meet you next time.' Well we used to do that for him. He knew we had some bantam fowls, and he used to say, 'I'll give you some wheat for your fowls when we meet next, if you'll give me some coal,' because that's what we carried.

We used to take 50 ton of coal down Frogmoor to the British Paper Mills, you had to throw it out by hand with a shovel. Well it was hard work for your wife, but she used to do it with you. Sometimes I'd ask a lad off another pair of boats to give me a hand, and we'd throw this 50 ton of coal out in a day. Well you earned six pounds for that, so I'd have three pounds and give him the other three pounds, and you was both happy with that.

After you'd done that you got to wash all your boats down, because they was all full of coal dust. You'd never travel with a pair of dirty boats, so you'd have to mop them up so you could go back nice and clean.

The things you would say when you was boating to each other, when you was

John Blunn on motor *Tiger*, behind butty *Warwick*, at Braunston locks 1958

going up the locks, and you was shutting the gates behind the boats and your wife was ready to draw the paddles, you'd shout, 'Get 'em up,' and if the boat got caught under the gate you'd shout, 'Drop 'em.' People who heard you would think you were being dirty, but it was the way to communicate fast with each other. It meant getting the paddle wound up or closing them fast in an emergency.

We was Barlowing at Croxley Mill, waiting to unload with about three or four pairs in front of us unloading, and one of the captains, Arthur Reddy, him and his wife worked together. His wife went off to the shops and she never returned. She had got on the train and went to Middlewich back to her mother. Well, he was panicking, and eventually he found out where she'd gone, and he had to work the boats back. He worked on the Grand Union for British Waterways.

Mary by *Warwick*, waiting to load at Baddesley, Atherstone, 1958

When you was going down the Grand Union Canal and there was only the two of you, you'd have the boats breasted up, because you couldn't open the gates and jump on the boat as the locks were too deep and there was no lock ladder in them days. You had a method using a short rope from each of the boat's masts, go round the gates, onto the handrail, and when you went in reverse when the lock was empty, it'd pull the gates open. When you went out of the lock, you'd have the rope looped in such a way it would slip off. You'd done that at every lock, and was something you'd work out for yourself, if you couldn't be on the bank.

Between locks, you'd clean your brasses as well as steering the boat, and mop off the roof, so your boats would always be nice and clean. You might be washing some ropes or making a fender - always something as well as steering the boat. You kept your mind and body active all the time.

The other places that you had to throw the coal out with a shovel was Home Park and Rugby. When we went to Home Park with two lots of coal, I'd get one of the lads there to help me. Ernie Grantham would sometimes help. Again, you'd give them half of the money, and if they wanted a hand with anything, well the same applied, and they'd share their money with you.

One day we was coming towards Ironbridge Lock near Watford, and when we got to the lock the Police were there. They said to us, 'You can go through, but take it gentle as we have just pulled a woman out of the canal and we are not sure yet whether there is anybody else in there. We just can't tell yet, because sometimes lovers or man and wife end it together.' We never heard any more about it, so we didn't know if they did find anybody else and we didn't have time to wait and find out.

One day we got to Sutton Stop and Mary's granddad was waiting on the lockside. He said to Mary, 'Can I come with you and John?' So he come with us for a while. Later on, as we came to the top of Stoke Bruerne, Sister Mary Ward come and told my Mary that her mother were very ill. So Mary went to see her mother, and when she got there, she took one look at her and said, 'You are coming with us.' That meant more work for Mary, but she gave her a bath, put her to bed looked after her and got her well After that, her granddad and mother had a single motor running from Coventry to Banbury, and me and Mary was on our own again.

Then in 1957 Mary became pregnant, so when she got near her time we stopped at Sutton Stop. Mary went into labour, and the ambulance took her to Golston Road Hospital and she had the baby next morning. She gave birth to our first son, John William, on the 9th March 1958. After that, working the boats was much harder with a baby to look after. The three of us would go all the way down to London and back, and we never shied away from the work. But if we could avoid having loads where you had to throw it out with a shovel, we did so! You would go to Apsley, Kings Langley, Croxley or the Jam 'ole, as they would empty your boats with a crane. That way it would give the wife time to do some washing and clean up before you started back again.

When we had our first baby, life working on the Grand Union was even harder. There was plenty of other couples in the same position, and we'd get some help from boats with bigger crews. If the Whitlocks came behind you, we used to let them past, as they could go faster than us. When you did that, their two children, Michael and Joan, would leave the locks set ready for you, so you would be almost as fast as them. This was a great help, and, even though it didn't happen

John Blunn at Braunston, 1958

every trip, you were grateful when it did and we always got on well with that family.

We got on well with most people. We'd have the odd row with some families if they drawed a lock up on us. We'd never fight with people like some of them did. I remember a couple of captains fighting over something, bashing hell out of each other. Mind you, they'd still have to pass each other most weeks, but that's how people went on. Have a fight, and then make it up.

When you was travelling on the Grand Union Canal, and one of you wasn't very well, you'd stop at Stoke Bruerne and you'd go and see the nurse, Sister Mary Ward, who lived by the lock there and tended the boat people. She'd give you something for your illness, or, if it were serious, she'd arrange for you to go to hospital. Mind you, you didn't get ill very often when boating as a rule, as you was out in all weathers, and you became hardened to a lot life threw at you.

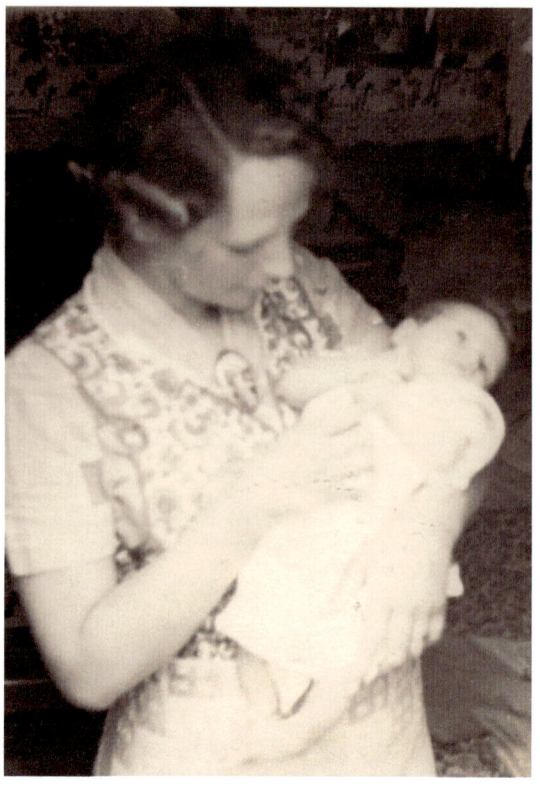

Mary with baby John

When you got to Sutton Stop, and there was a few pairs of boats there, you'd go in the Greyhound and have a drink, and a good old sing song. There was some that could play the accordion. You'd have a good time, as you had to take your entertainment when you could, as you'd always be off bright and early next morning. I was not a big drinker, but I have seen some boatmen, at closing time, go and fetch the water cans and have them filled with beer. They'd then carry on drinking through the night, until they ran out.

Chapter 8

A life on the Bank

After about 18 months of that, we decided we would try and get off the boats so that our children would have some schooling. So me and Mary and her mother and granddad bought a houseboat at Sutton Stop, and lived on that for a while. Then we bought a caravan from Albert and Violet Beechey at Longford. Joe Skinner and Sid Givens helped us to pull the houseboat from Sutton Stop to Longford to get our things off to put in the caravan. We lived in that and we was very happy. I got a job at the GEC, but I had to bike six miles at each end of the day and the money was not much good, so I looked for another job closer to home because, by this time, Mary was pregnant again. I ended up with a job working for a timber company that was only a mile and a half from home.

Mary had another son, Michael, on the 28th of January 1960. Now the caravan was too small for the four of us. I was telling one of the lads at work about it, and he told me about this company that had got houses. He said, 'I live in one of their houses just up the road and the one next door is empty. Why don't you see them?' So I did and I got it. When I got home and told Mary she was over the moon about it.

We lived there for about 2 years and then we got a council house at Bell Green, Henley Road - a nice house even though it were on a main road, but we was happy there. I left my job and got another one in an engineering factory, packing up machinery to go all over the country. It was a good job, but I was like a bird in a cage after being on the canals all my life, so I looked for something with a bit of interest to it. You don't want to be penned up in a factory, unless you really have to.

I got a job working for Bootle and Normans, a woodworking machinery firm. I liked this job because they looked up to my abilities, and gave me a free hand, after they had showed me what wanted doing. They'd give me a drawing and showed me how to set the machine up, and then they would leave me to it. I don't know what would have happened if I had got it wrong because I don't have any skills in wood-working machinery, but they gave me a chance to show my ability, and I come through it with flying colours. The foreman come to me afterwards and said, 'John, you did alright. Me and the boss were saying to each other after we give you the job, he will do it, he looks educated.' Little did they know that I had never been to school!

Mary got a part time job in Henley College, where she used to go in at 6 am in the morning until 8 am, which was good as she was always back to take the children to school. The children would come home for dinner them days, if the school was close enough. Then Mary would pick them up at night, and as I would be home from work by then, Mary would have given them their tea, then she would go to work from 6 pm until 8 pm. She would never leave the children with anyone but me. She used to say, 'They are our children and we are responsible for them growing up into good adults.' She was right in every word she said because, looking at my sons and daughter now, they are all married and got families of their own; they are good people. You only get out of a family what you put into it, and I hope they do the same for their families.

Mary worked at Henley College for a long time, until she had a row with the caretaker, when she told him to stick his job and walked out. He sent another woman after her to ask her to come back, but not Mary, no way. If you upset her that was it, full stop. We had lived in Henley for about seven years, and then we had another baby, a little girl, Kathleen Angela Annette. She was a bundle of joy. We always said if we had any more children we would like a daughter, and our wish came true.

The day she was supposed to arrive, she was late. Mary told me in the night she was starting, so I jumped out of bed and got the car out of the garage, expecting Mary to be ready, but she said, 'I am going to have a cup of tea before I go. You may not get one up there.' I was panicking a bit by now, but the baby didn't arrive until the afternoon after all. I phoned up and they gave me the good news. I took the boys up to the hospital that night to see their Mum and little sister and they ate all Mary's custard creams. Then I took them over to the club and got them some pop and crisps. When Mary came home with the baby, I had got the place all nice and clean and a pot of tea and a plate of cakes ready for her. You know, she never forgot that, as she very often said how nice it was.

Michael and John were always forbidden to cross the main road to go to the playing fields. But about a year after Kathy was born, the lad next door went across and Michael followed him. A car hit Michael, but it was not the driver's fault. Thankfully he was only driving slow, or it would have killed him. Me and the neighbour took him to the hospital, but he was only badly bruised. After that, Mary didn't want to stay in that house any longer, so we decided to try and get a house in the country near the canal, and we both started going off with the children looking for a place. We got talking to a man who knew us and our families. His name was Sammy Lomas, and he lived at Autherley Junction near Wolverhampton, and was connected with British Waterways. He said to us, 'You leave it with me and I will see what I can do.' A week later, we had a letter telling us to go to Ellesmere and meet Mr Jim Howard, the inspector of the canal there. He had a house and a job, but after we had seen it we turned it down. It was not the right place for the children's schooling. We wrote to Sammy Lomas telling him this house didn't suit us and thanking him for letting us know about it.

A few weeks later we had another letter off him telling us there was another house coming empty at Wheaton Aston. He said, 'Go to Norbury on Monday and see Inspector Bill Dean.' We knew Mr Dean from when we was boating for Thomas Clayton down the Shropshire Union Canal in our younger days, so off we went to see him. He said right away, 'You can have the house and the job. I need a good chap to go piling with Tommy Trew,' who I already knew and liked, as he was a very nice man.

We used to come down from Coventry to Wheaton Aston every weekend on a Saturday with the boys, leaving Kathy with Mary's mum for the day. We had to clean the house up at Wheaton Aston because a dirty family had it before us. Me and Mary worked hard doing it up, painting and decorating and getting the place nice and clean so we could move in. I gave my job up in the wood-working factory, and they said they understood why I was going, but if I ever wanted a job at any time there would be a job for me with them. We booked a furniture van and started to pack all our things ready for the moving date. We moved to Wheaton Aston on Thursday 15th January 1970. Waterways said to me, 'You can stop at Wheaton Aston on Friday to put your furniture right and we will pick you up 7.30 am Monday morning,' - so I was back on the canals again. We had already fixed the boys up for school, Johnny had to go to Wolgarston school in Penkridge on the school bus, and Michael went to the primary school in Wheaton Aston.

When we moved from Coventry, we had to take Mary's mother with us because she lived on her own in a flat in Coventry and we couldn't leave her there. So as there were her belongings as well as ours, we had quite a load. When we got all the things in the furniture van we set off. We could not get everyone in our car, so Johnny went in the furniture van with the men and they followed us. When we got there, Mary had lit a fire and made a cup of tea. Now we were in our new home near the canal again, something we had missed all those years.

It's funny, but even when we lived in Coventry, we always had a holiday on the canal. We used to hire a boat from Ernest Thomas and we really used to enjoy it. We was going up Atherstone Locks on one holiday, and our John, he was only about seven, asked if he could take the boat up the pound to the next lock. I let him take the boat and stopped on the bank with Mary.

The pound was a bit low, so I told to him to keep her in the channel, the middle of the canal where it's deepest. He set off alright, but when he was halfway up the pound he got stuck, and he didn't know how to get the boat off the bottom. So I said to him, 'Throw me the rope', meaning throw me one end of the rope leaving the other end attached to the boat, but instead he threw me the whole rope! I says to him 'You stupid little sod.' I was jumping up and down in temper on the bank. Mary was laughing, saying, 'It's your fault for letting him take the boat on his own.' He also learned a lesson - he never did it again!

Now we were living at Wheaton Aston, it was time for me and Mary to get going on the garden and the house. Mary could make any old thing look like new. She used to get a joy out of it, because all our lives we had to make do and mend. Then one day I had to take an old icebreaker boat down the canal to be broken up, because it was rotten. The cabin was almost new, so I asked the boss if I could have it, not the boat just the cabin, and he said, 'Yes if you get it off at the weekend.' So me and the boys went up to the lock on Saturday morning with my tools and we got it off and carried it down home, and I made a strong shed out of it. Then I put a bench and a vice and some shelves in and had myself a nice workshop. I would spend hours in there making things.

Piling on the Stafford and Worcester Canal

Mary loved her garden. She used to say, 'You are closer to God in a garden.' One day, the policeman, who lived next door, asked her if she would like to be a lollypop lady *(school crossings supervisor)* as they had never had one before at Wheaton Aston. He says, 'If you want it, I can get it for you.' She said, 'I'll give it a try,' and she did it for over 20 years!

When we got some money, we saved it up and managed to buy a 30 foot Springer boat. We kept it on the moorings just below Wheaton Aston Lock, and used to go out on it every weekend, and had a lovely time on the boat. Later on, we sold that one, and bought another, so we was never without a boat. We would do them up and sell them to get a bigger one.

Me and Mary worked hard together. When the boat wanted painting, we did it together. Mary always felt safe when we was together.

When John left school, I got him a job on British Waterways. He served an apprenticeship as a carpenter from 1974. He had to go to Luton sixteen weeks every year for college and he didn't like being away from home. He still works for Waterways now, so I suppose it's in the blood.

After our two sons and daughter got married, Mary gave up her job as lollypop lady and about twelve months later I took early retirement when I was 60. We went to live on the boat and had a good holiday. Well I say holiday - but it involved doing jobs on the boat too. We pretty near did the whole canal system in the next few years!

After a while, we decided to get a place by the canal so we bought a place in Penkridge in 1994. We had not been living there long before our son's marriage broke up, and as he had four children, he asked us to help him out. Mary and I looked after the children for six years, then, as they got older, we had a bit more freedom to go boating again.

Me and Mary liked to get away weekends from home. We used to go to West Bromwich to my sister's one weekend then we would go to my other sister's at Chester or we would go to Middlewich to my sister there. Sometimes we would go to Coventry to the sister-in-law or we would go to the seaside for the weekend. We would go anywhere to get away from home, because if you was at home someone would want you. Now Mary is not with me I don't go away so often. It's not the same on your own.

End of a partnership

We enjoyed several happy years in this way, until 2004, when Mary was taken ill. In April, she was taken into hospital. They did some tests and found a tumour on the brain. That turned our world upside down because they told us there was no cure, but with an operation it would give her longer to live. It was a very hard decision to make. In May 2004, they said

Mary loved gardening - Wheaton Aston

John, Mary and daughter Kath, 1981

that if she didn't have the operation she would only last two months, so we gave them the permission to operate and she had it done on the 4th June 2004. I had her home on the 17th June and looked after her for almost six months, 24 hours a day. It was hard going, not looking after her but, knowing that it was only a limited time, it was a big strain on all of us. Our children helped me as much as they could, what with their jobs and families to look after, and they were there when I needed them right to the end.

Mary's end was very sad. On the 2nd December 2004 Mary passed away peacefully. My life has been up and down since then. She was part of my life and I miss her more than words can say. Life is never going to be the same again without her. She was the backbone of the family and we all miss her very much - God bless her.

Life is different when you are on your own. You have got time to think, and you think about what you could have done to make her much happier and the things you did that you shouldn't have done, and the things you used to say to her that you are sorry for now. I suppose that's what you call true love, though. The saying is, 'You always hurt the one you love', and now I am hurt because I have lost her. Everything I do now is for Mary. I breath because it's what Mary would want me to do. I live because it's what Mary would like me to do. I eat because Mary would want me to eat. I know she's not here, but sometimes I feel she is saying this wants doing, that wants doing, like she used to do, but now I cannot answer back. Life must go on. Mary used to say life is for living, so now I must look after what Mary has left behind and do the things she used to do, like home work, washing and painting and decorating and gardening.

Mary was not only a good wife. She was a good mother and grandmother and a lovely person. She could get on with anyone, bringing out the best in people and getting them talking. You could get on a train or a bus or walking, and before long Mary would be talking to someone. People like that, but it takes guts to start a conversation with strangers. Mary

Morning Star outside our home in Penkridge in 1995

could do that and before the end of the journey they was thanking her for talking to them. You would be surprised how people would open up to you and tell you all about their troubles and their joys. But Mary used to say we are all brothers and sisters in God's eyes.

Back to boating

We always loved the canal life, so I am getting back on the canals whenever I can. Mary's funeral was a very sad occasion, but lots of friends and family came along, showing how much they all loved Mary. An old friend, Mavis Waldron, who had not long before lost her husband Jack, and her daughter Lucy (Waldron as now is) asked me if I'd like to take their old little Woolwich motor, *Cepheus*, out. I first took it out on the 12th July 2005 and took Mavis with me. Mary and I had known Mavis and her husband Jack ever since we first come to Wheaton Aston. Lucy and our daughter, Kath, were about the same age, and had played together as children. Jack and Mavis had lived up at the Lock and had old working boats before. Both of us really enjoyed our day out, and got back about 5.30 pm.

I know now that the good things in life never last for long, so you must enjoy every moment. I borrowed *Cepheus* again on the 21st July, this time I took Kath with me. We went to Norbury and met John and his daughter and had lunch together. We got back about 7.30 pm and Mark, Kath's husband, met us with the boys, so I gave them a ride on the boat. They enjoyed that. We went out more times after this, taking Kath and her three boys with us for a picnic. I let my grandson Thomas take the tiller, but only when I was close by him, and going very gentle! Since then, we've had lots of days out with the boat, either me and Mavis or with

John, Mary and grandson Thomas

family. It's more fun when there is others to share the day with. In August 2005, as a special treat, me and Thomas stayed on the boat for the night. On Friday we went to the bottom of the Wolverhampton 21 to turn around, then we set off back. Thomas was overjoyed because he had slept on a workboat, and he had done something his granddad and grandmother and all his family had done so many years before. He loves boats, does Thomas.

I've been helping with *Stour*, an old Clayton's boat too - down at the Black Country Living Museum in Dudley. Lucy and her husband helped do it up for the museum a few years before, and it was the last Bolinder engine her dad, Jack, had worked on with her and Joe Hollingshead. In 2006, the tar boat butty, *Gifford*, went to the rally up the Crow *(Titford)* pulled by a horse, and we took the *Stour* and *Cepheus* up there too. We was all moored up in a line, with Grand Union boats on the outside. *Stour* was used to take *Gifford* back to the Port *(the Boat Museum at Ellesmere Port),* and I steered all the way back. Who'd have thought after all these years, I'd be captain of a Clayton's pair again on the Port run? It makes you think – you're never too old to get up and do things, even if life has knocked you back some. The boats and canals have helped me keep going after losing Mary. It's helped me remember

John Blunn on *Cepheus*

the good times me and her had together when we worked on the boats, and the people we met and the fun we had.

There was lots of satisfaction being on the canal. The freedom you got, doing what you wanted to do, and being your own boss. You had to do your trip as quickly as possible, and make sure the company was happy with your work, but that was it really. The sad thing is that the women didn't get paid anything, even though they worked harder than the men. They had to work the boats with the men, as well as do the cooking, washing and cleaning and look after the children. Would many women do that today? Probably not, and probably rightly too.

When my grandchildren and their children and grandchildren read this, I hope they are proud of it, as proud as I am writing it. If I lived my life all over over again I wouldn't change a thing.

John Blunn steering the family boat, the former Midlands & Coast owned *The North*, built in 1925.
Photo: Ian Saunders

Chapter 9

Marriage to Mavis

Mavis Waldron and her daughter Lucy Waldron came to Mary's funeral, as they was good friends of me and my wife and family for years. Lucy and Mavis thought that I would just give up, knowing how close me and my wife was. So they asked me would I like to look after Lucy's boat *Cepheus* as Lucy was living in New Zealand. She wanted someone she could trust, and knew my canal knowledge. She was happy knowing her boat would be in good hands and it made me think that life must go on, as also the love I have got for the canal. I knew my wife Mary would want me to.

As time passed, I asked Mavis if she would like to come out on the boat for a trip to Norbury. She came on a few trips, then we started to go to boat rallies, and we got on well together. We both knew that we would not go anywhere on our own. We never looked back. We grew very fond of each other; we go to about six boat rallies a year.

As time went on, we decided to sell my park home at Penkridge, and I moved in with Mavis at Wheaton Aston. We was very happy together, so we decided to get married, which we did in August 2015.

Gertrude at Sutton Stop, 1958

Additional Notes for Second Edition

Written in 2016, these notes amplify some earlier chapters,
but also provide further information

My Father and Mother got married in Wolverhampton. After they married, they set off the same day down Wolverhampton locks, and moored up at Coven outside the Anchor pub. It is called the Fox and Anchor now; it was just the Anchor then. Them days, the pub had stables for the horses. The next morning, they set off early. They would do long hours, so they could stable their horse for the night. They would set off early the next morning. As time went by, they started a family; over a number of years, the family got bigger, they had five daughters and then they had a boy, which was me. And then they had another daughter, and later on they had another boy, making a total of eight children. By then, they had two horse boats, so had a man friend to work the other horse boat, because the girls were not old enough to work the horse. The friend's name was Billy Powell, a good friend of the family. He once saved my life, as when I was only two years old I tipped out of the hatches into the river. Billy Powell was a good swimmer; he jumped in the river and saved me. When I grew up I meant to thank him, but I never got the chance, because one day going down Cheshire Locks, there was a cable going across the towpath; it must have been live, and it killed him, poor man.

When my Father had the horse boats, he sometimes had to walk behind the horse all the way from Birmingham to Manchester, if he had a horse that would not go on its own. Some horses, if you got on the boat to have a sandwich and a cup of tea, the horse would stop and look round, so you would have to get off the boat with a cup of tea and sandwich and walk behind the horse, and eat it. Because there was a lot of horse boats in them days on the canals, and you had to be on the bank with the horse when you was passing another horse boat coming the other way, if your boat was empty and the other boat was loaded. The man with the loaded boat would stop his horse and let the empty boat horse walk over his line, then the empty boat would clear the line over the loaded boat That way, both boats could carry on without delay. But if you was meeting a motor and butty, you would stay on the towpath side. But normally in them days you would pass each other on the left but now you pass on the right. Even in those days if you had a horse boat, you would pass on the side that the towpath was on if you was meeting a motor and butty, because your horse would be on the towpath side so that's the side you would pass on.

Later on as the family grew older, my Mother and Father gave up the horse boats and had a motor and butty. That way you didn't have to walk behind the horse. But you still had things to do like keeping the engine running. Every morning you had to make sure that the engine had got enough oil and diesel to last all day and every day, because if your engine breaks down, you would have to moor up and send for the fitter and that would take a day and maybe it would need spare parts, that is if you could not fix it yourself, it could take another day, so it may delay you for a couple of days. Then you was losing money. Them days, if you didn't work you didn't get paid, not like it is today. It was your responsibility to get from one end of the canal to the other in the shortest possible time. You didn't do that for one week - you had to do it year in, year out. That's why you didn't get much schooling, or for a better word education. You was not in one place long enough. You had to help with the working of the boats with your parents. If you was at one of the towns like Manchester, Wolverhampton, Birmingham, Nottingham or Chester, if you was spending a night in one of the towns, you would have a wash and change, and go to the pictures. That was the only luxury you had, but it made you a better person. You didn't have much money, so what you had you looked after. Today, the kids don't know the value of money. Yes, they have the education, but that does not make them better than us. We had more freedom; the more freedom you get, the more you learn about the countryside and nature. Some of the kids today don't know where milk comes from, because the schools don't teach enough about the countryside and nature. When we was kids, and the boats was travelling between locks, us kids would get off onto the bank and walk for miles. We would walk in the woods, and when we got to the locks, we would help with the gates. We only did the paddles when we got older.

My eldest got married to Joe Theobald, and they had a horse boat for Thomas Clayton. The girls got older and each one got a boyfriend and got married, and they too had a Thomas Clayton horse boat. Each one got married, and made their own way in life, and had their own families. As each left home, things got harder for my Father loading the boats. When he had to load two boats with two hundred weight bags of sugar at Ellesmere Port, he had to lift every bag off the bank and stack them in the boat, loading two boats in one day, then take it right up to Wolverhampton and empty them.

Then he was asked to work for Thomas Clayton of Oldbury, so he took up the offer and things got easier for him because he didn't have to lift heavy goods any more. Thomas Clayton didn't carry goods, they only carried crude oil and tar and creosote, so all you that had to do was pull the lead up and put the pipe in the boat, and they pumped the oil in; the same when you got to the place where you had got to empty it. You put the pipe in and they pumped it out, so it was so much easier for my dad. If he had things easier in

Mavis and John on *The North.*   Photo: Ian Saunders

his early life, maybe he would have lived longer, but you can't turn the clock back. You have to face whatever life throws at you; when you are young, you don't realise how hard it is for your parents. They worry about the family and how to keep them safe. They have to work long hours, and then when I got older and had to work a horse boat with my Mother and young brother after my dad died, there was no one but me to help to keep food on the table. It was my responsibility to look after the horse and boat, and I was only 17 years old at the time. My mother would get me up in the morning early. I would go to the stable, get the horse ready, and get the line off the boat and peg it to the horse, then we would set off to get our load - go down Smethwick then down Farmers Bridge 13 locks, then down Aston 11 locks, then we got our load, we'd go all the way back to Oldbury and empty the boat, put the horse back in the stable and feed him and get him ready for the next morning, and do the same again next day.

I have gone down Farmers Bridge in the dark in a morning and also down Aston locks. We didn't set off too early every morning; sometimes we would set off a bit later so that it would be daylight by the time we got to the locks. One day we was going down Aston locks, we met another boat coming the other way. As we were entering the lock, the back water sent us into the lock so fast, mother put the rope round the gate head and she lapped it around the boats stud. She got her two fingers in the way, and it cut two of the end of her fingers off, so we had to take her to the hospital. That delayed us for a few hours, so when we got back to Oldbury the boss said your mum can't work the locks with her hand like that, so I going to let you do local trips until your mum gets better. That way she only had to steer the boat. The boss always has you interests at heart, because they knew if everything was going alright you would do your job and you would look after the boats and horses. I worked the horse boats with my mum until she said she had decided to call it a day. She wanted to finish with the boats, so she and my young brother went to Middlewich to live with my sister and her husband. I stayed with Thomas Clayton; they gave me a boat called the *Dart*, it had a 15 horse Bolinder in. I worked a trip a day from Oldbury to the gas works in Wolverhampton locks and back to Oldbury every day, 5 days a week. I did that for about 18 months.

Every weekend I would get a train to Coventry to see my girlfriend; she worked for Samuel Barlow's, but I always had to go back Sunday afternoon. I had to get two buses and a train to get back to Oldbury ready for work next morning. I did that most weekends, so one day I gave up working for Clayton's and got a job with Samuel Barlow's. I took the motor boat Betty, and when me and my girlfriend got married, we had two boats, a motor and butty. We used to carry coal from the Coventry area to London. We did that for about three years, by this time we started a family. We had our first child, a boy, so things got harder for us, and the carrying we could see was slowing down. We bought a place at Longford, Coventry, and gave up the boats and went to live on the bank. It was not the same as boating. I got a job, and later we had another son and daughter. Later, my wife got a job, but we still used to have a holiday on the canal because that was our life we were used to. We lived at Bell Green, Henley Road, for 11 years but we never settled living near a main road, and when our Mike got hit by a car, Mary never settled there, after that Mike could have been killed that day. So we started looking around for somewhere else to live near the canal. We had a few offers, but they were not what we were looking for. We were offered a house and job at Ellesmere working for British Waterways, but we turned it down. The house was alright, and the job, but my wife could not drive, and she would have to walk about two miles to take the children to school morning and night. Then we was offered a house at Walsall with a job, but we didn't want to live in Walsall. So we turned that down as well. We didn't think we would be offered another one, but in the early days British Waterways gave ex-canal men a chance. They would take you on because the boat men were hard workers with experience on canals. Waterways employed a lot of ex-boat men after they finished with the working boats. After I finished with the working boats, I made my own way in life. I got a job at the GEC working outside in the gardening and cricket ground. It didn't pay much, and I had to bike six miles each end of the day, so I looked around for a better job near home, and that paid well. I never left a job until I got another one. I did get another job; it paid well and you could do overtime so it got you more money. The hours didn't bother because you was used to it. You did longer hours

The North tied up at Audlem in July 2011 alongside Nick & Liz Grundy's *Beatty* - a boat which John Blunn worked in the 1950s for Samuel Barlow.   Photo: David Williams

when you was working the boats and there was one working for it because, when you was working the boat, all the family was working the boat but only the captain was paid.

Getting back to BWB, they did offer me another house and a job. The house was at Wheaton Aston, and the job was on the canal. They gave me the motor boat *Scorpio*, and the job was driving steel piles to put the towpath back in good condition, and also the offside of the canal. Over the years the farms had lost a lot of land with the wash from the boats. So it had to be put back again. So I would be sent to a selected site to pile it and then the dredger would come along and backfill it to give the farmer his land back. When the land gets washed away, the canal gets wider, and the Shropshire Union should be only 40ft., and the Stafford and Worcester only 38 ft. Its things like the land getting washed away that fills the canal up with silt, then it needs to be dredged. Back in the early days, the canals were always dredged, but as the budget got tighter, the canals didn't get dredged, so after the early 1990s, only spot dredging. That is, only bridge holes and lock entrances, so there is nowhere for the mud in the main channels to go. Years ago they would dredge the winding holes, so there was somewhere that the mud could go out of the main channel; now they don't even do that. Now the farmers don't let the canal have a bit of land to use as a tip like they used to because of toxic waste. But you only get toxic waste in the built up area where there are factories, so the canals don't get dredged. I was working for BWB for 24 years, and I did a lot of piling in that time, towpath and offside, and also between locks.

I enjoyed my time back on the canals, and even when I worked on the canals in the week, we always had our own boat, so when I finished work on a Friday night, me and my wife would go out for the weekend. We didn't go far, we just got away from home, but we was always back Sunday night so I could go to work on Monday morning. Then we would do the same the next weekend, and that's the way it was almost every weekend until I retired, then me and my wife had 18 months on the boat fitting it out. Then we bought a park home in Penkridge by the Stafford and Worcester Canal, and I lived there for 18 years. I had eight years on my own after I lost my wife in 2004. Then I sold the park home in 2012, and moved back to Wheaton Aston.

Me and my new wife Mavis still go to a few boat rallies every year, we do most of the repairs ourselves on the boat, and in the house and garden, and we hope to do so for a long time to come, God willing. Me and Mavis share an age of 165 years. I guess we have been lucky. We have put a new bath and shower with mixer taps and sink with cupboard in our boat, and tiled it throughout. Now we have got to do the outside jobs after the winter, ready for Easter at Ellesmere Port. That's what keeps us going.

I remember when my father was working for Fellows Morton, we was going along the Birmingham main line to Birmingham with two loaded boats. When we go to Winson Green Stop, there was a horse boat loaded with some cargo. My father was near the stop place. This joey boat kept coming and jammed my father's boat in the stop place. Him and my father was arguing. He said he was not going back with his boat. My father said he was not going back, so the man on the horse boat said 'ok, we will fight for it'. My father took his coat off, jumped on the bank, and said 'come on then, the best man wins'. Then the man on the horse boat said 'ok, forget it, I will go back'. From then on, they was always friendly with my father. My father didn't want to fight over the right of way, but if he didn't get on the bank, they would have told all the other boatmen that my father was a coward, then they would have picked on him. But from then on, the other boaters respected my father. There was times when you had to give or take, or fight for rights. Some you would win, some you would lose, but it made you harder. Some time you would fight, the next minute you would buy one another pint. There was no bitterness between you because each one of you had a job to do, so you got on with it. But Sam Lomas (*toll collector at Cut End – Autherley Junction*) was right – you can do what you like with another man's wife, but keep your hands off, she's mine. Joe Green used to say if you have a large family, when they grow up the less work you would have to do. It's like the boat women; they would fall out over the kids fighting, then if you had got any trouble, they would be there to help you.

One morning when I was horse boating with my mother, I set off at 3.00 am from Oldbury to go to Windsor Street, part way down the Ashton locks, to load. When I got the horse to the boat, I pegged the line on the horse, and put him through the Anchor bridge. I would get on the boat and have a cup of tea and a piece of cake till I got to the turnover bridge. Then I would stay with him all round Spon Lane, then I would get back on the boat along Sandwell, till I got to the bridge above Smethwick. Then I would get the bike off, go and get the three locks ready, and be back at the top lock for when the horse and boat got there. As it was black dark, you had to be very careful. You had to look after the horse, the boat and yourself, and them that was on the boat. We was going down Smethwick, when up comes another boat, chasing us. It was Billy Beech and Joe Chitten. They didn't like it because we started before them. They was trying to get past us. Joe Chitten ripped a paddle up as we was going out of the lock. As he ripped the paddle up, it sent the helm over, and almost knocked my mother into the cut, out of the hatches. That made me lose my temper, so I stopped the horse. I ran back to Joe Chitten; I gave him a right old blocking. I came very near to hitting him. They kept well back from then on. After that, me and Joe Chitten was good friends; we still are every time we meet up. He's never forgot – he brings it up and tells anybody about it. That's how it was them days, with you losing your temper you could have killed each other. There was boatmen killed by fighting over locks, and things like that. I remember two boatmen fighting over a lock at Whartons Lock. They was fighting, and one of them hit the other and knock him backwards down the steps. He must have him hard, and it killed him. But the other man didn't have to go to jail because the man that was killed was a trouble maker. He had been falling out with everybody up and down the cut. I do know the name of the man that killed the other man, but I am not going to name him.

I was only 17 years of age when I had to take charge of a horse and boat, and look after my mother and my young brother. It was going ok until they called me up for the Army. I passed, so I had to go. That meant that my mother and young brother could not work the horse and boat. That meant they could not get a living without me, so my mother had to go all over the place to try and get me back out of the Army. This took a long time. I was doing my training, and as I got to the end of my training, they was going to send us to fight in Korea.

If I had gone to Korea, I may not have been around now to tell the story. I didn't want to come out of the army, but my mother needed me to work the horse and boat. Two of my boating mates had to go to Korea, and one of them got blew up in an ammunition wagon. He was not killed, but he never walked again, and that was in 1952. The other lad didn't get injured, but the one that got blew up is in a wheelchair from that day onwards. My mother getting me out of the Army may have been for the best.

It is lovely to see some of the working boats being looked after. Owners of the working boats now, like Sarah Edgson, the Pinnocks, Blossom, David Ray, Paul Barber, Malcolm Burge, Laurence Williams, Roger Hatchard, Roger and Teresa Fuller, Matt and Rebekah Parrott, Mick Poyser, Nick and Liz Grundy, Andrew Hoyle and lots of others are all good friends of mine, but they are not working the boats like we used to. After work, some carry items like coal, diesel, gas and other things. But we had to do it every week, work long hours, week in week out. A lot of work boating fiends will tell you the same. The working boatmen that are still alive are Roger and Jean Hatchard, Ron and Brenda Withy, John and Phil Saxon, Henry and Phyllis Johnson, Fred Bunn, Joe Hollingshead, Henry Hollingshead, John Brooks, Eddie and Jim Hambridge, George Carter, Laura Carter, Martha Nixon, Tommy Lapworth, Alice Lapworth, George Wain, and my three sisters Helen Clowes, Doris Green and Violet Appleton. But working boatmen are now thin on the ground. We have just lost one very good friend, a good boatman, Fred Heritage. The reason that I am writing all this down is that there has been too many boatmen and women that have passed away, and took all that knowledge with them.

My father and mother could not read or write, but could handle money and work hard day and night. Sometimes they would have a fly load, so they would get it to the depot in the shortest possible time – so it was long days. Now you know what boat people had to do to get a living. Joe Safe once told me that he and his wife Polly had to get two fly loads from Brentford to Birmingham. He and his wife put their shoes on at Brentford and they went off, never stopped till they got to Birmingham, and had blisters on their feet. They then went to the coalfields to pick up two loads of coal for Croxley – and a lot more boat men and women did the same. The only rest the boat people got is when they had to stop for stoppages, and then they would have a good clean up on the boats, ready for when the stoppages was over.

My father and mother had to work all night sometimes. When I was horse boating, one day I was coming from Swan Village with a load on, when I noticed the horse was pulling to the one side as if he was in pain or something, so I stopped the horse. I lifted his collar up and I could see why he was pulling to one side. The collar had been rubbing his shoulder tender, so I put a pad in between his collar and his shoulder, so I could get him to Oldbury to get it attended to – as Thomas Clayton had a man working for them that mixed the corn for the horses, and he looked after horses. Thomas Clayton had a lot of horses, so if your horse got lame, you could leave your horse in the stable and take another one out, that gave your horse a chance to recover. Getting back to my horse's bad shoulder, I get in to Oldbury, and take the horse to the stable. I took off the harness, and gave him a feed of corn and a drink of water. Then I go and see the man that looks after the horses and tell him about the bad shoulder on the horse. The words he used was "piss on it". I was a bit taken aback with what he said, so I asked him again what he meant; he said it again, 'piss on it'. I said that I won't, that would make it painful. He said there is something in the urine that heals wounds. He said to leave him here for a few days, so I said 'will you pull the collar in for me?' If a horse has got a bad shoulder, you can pull the collar in around the wound. You use a needle and thread, and you pull like a hole in the padding around the wound, so the padding doesn't touch the open wound, and then it gives it a chance to heal up. Yes, it did work; the horse never had a bad shoulder again. They say it's hard on the shoulder, so it does not rub the shoulder around the weak area.

Thomas Claytons had some nasty horses. There was one that my brother-in-law had – he would run at you with an open mouth, and if he caught you he would bite you. Some horses would kick out at you. I had a horse that kicked a boatman and broke his arm. But if you treat your horse right, he will do anything for you. Horses are like humans; you only get out of them what you put in. If you treat anybody with respect, they will treat you the same – and it's the same with horses.

There was someone once said to someone else that I had not done any boating. She told me and she said she will never forgive her for it, because she knows my history, and she said the reason she said it was that she was jealous, and she had too much to drink, and she didn't have the courage to say it to my face. But my history speaks for itself. I don't hold a grudge; I just feel sorry for people like that. She didn't know me when I was boating.

My mum and dad was boating all their lives, and they had some hard times with bringing the family up, and looking after their safety. With the hard winters we used to have, with working on the canals, there was always a danger everything was slippery; even the ropes was hard as steel. You could never lap the ropes up. And when you did pull them out of the way, your hands would be that cold that you had hot aches in your fingers. A lot of people don't know that because they never work a pair of boats in the winter. Ice on the canal made boating very difficult. But you had to try and get through the ice if you could, but if the ice got too thick, you had to stop, otherwise you would damage your boats, especially with wooden boats. When you have gone through that for years and years, then you can say you are a boatman or woman – until then you are just a novice. I am sorry, but you are all good friends of mine, but I have got to get this over to them that think they know it all. I will help anybody that wants me to. Anything that they would like to know, if I know it I will pass it on. If I don't know it, I cannot tell you.

When I worked for British Waterways, I have worked with lots of men on different jobs, but my main job was steel piling bank protection. It was a two-man job. We have driven thousands of piles up and down the canal. It was not an easy job. One of you would have to stand in the water, and the other one would stand on the planks, with the jack hammer driven by a compressor. We would sometimes stand on the ice, and still drive the piles. The boss would say to go into the cabin and have a warm whenever you want to. Them days, you would do that, but in this day and age, you would not be allowed to that with Health & Safety so strong. But if we was waiting for piles to be delivered, we would cut some bushes off on the offside. The boss would say 'you know what wants doing, but you will have to make do with a bowsaw. I must not let you have a chainsaw; if I do, I will have no trees left!' That's how he was; you could have a laugh and a joke with him. It's not like that any more. If you know what to do, you are not allowed to do it until an engineer comes and says ok, you can do the job now. I think it was better in them days because you got on with the job and you didn't hold the boats up too long.

We was coming back from the Audlem Transport Festival in 2015; when we got to Woodseaves Cutting, there was a large tree fell across the canal. Me and twenty more was held up 26 hours; we had a night in there. I understand that they could not get a vehicle to the tree, so they had to bring a boat with all the tools on – chainsaws, and chains and ropes. When they did get the boat there, they was not long getting us away. We got going at 1.30pm the next day. That's how things work these days; when we used to work for British Waterways, there was always a dredger on the Shropshire Union Canal, then the dredger would be taken to where the tree came down. There would be men with chainsaws, who would cut the tree up, then the dredger driver would put the bucket under the cut up tree and lift it on to the bank. Thee there would be a way through for the boats, which would not be held up for too long – two to three hours at the most. When they was away through, the men with chainsaws would cut up the trees into logs.

My father was born in 1903, name John Henry Blunn, but better known as Jack. He was born illegitimately; his mother's name was Rose; she was our grandmother. She and her sister had illegitimate children. Her sister's son was named William, better known as Bill, so as they were not married, my father and his cousin had to take the name of Blunn, because their mothers were not married. As our names was Blunn, us kids always thought our father and Williams was brothers, but in later life we was told all about it. William's mother was named Jane. My mother was named Margaret Alice Jones before they was married. My mother's father was a boatman; him and my grandmother had three daughters and one son. Their names was Margaret, Alice, Ellen and Jane, and their son was Jack. My father and mother had eight children – six daughters and two boys. My Aunt Ellen and her husband had four boys – Albert, Arthur, Vernon and Alphie – and they had four daughters – Mary, Ellen, Jean and Dorothy. Then for some unknown reason they ended their marriage. My other Aunt, Jane, married Arthur Green, the brother of Joe Green who worked on the Grand Union Canal for Fellows, Morton & Clayton Ltd. He had the wooden motor boat *Daffodil*, brand new, built at Uxbridge.

Jack and Mavis Waldron became the new owners of *Daffodil* until she was resold, and then she sank and was broken up. When I finished boating for Samuel Barlow's, we bought a converted joey boat from Ron Wilson, ex-boatman. He lived in a house at Sutton Stop, on the offside by the lock, but it is not there anymore. It was demolished some time ago. I don't know why, you would never know there had ever been a house there. We bought this houseboat from Ron, and we lived on it for a while, and we had my wife's granddad living with us. There was lots of room in it, compared to a boat's back cabin, so we all lived comfortably until we bought a caravan off a friend of the family, Albert Beech. We sold the houseboat, and moved to Longford, off Lady Lane. The caravan site was alongside the canal, just across from where we used to load coal for the London area. As we had not long left the canal, it was good to be living so close to it. We had been on the canal for so long, it was in our blood.

Even after we had left the canal, we used to hire a boat for our holidays. I know it's funny – we had left the canal, and still wanted a holiday on the canal. As I said, the canal was in our blood, and it still is. We used to hire from Ernie Thomas at Calf Heath. He knew my father in mother in their younger days. He made us very welcome, because he had that trust in us, being experienced boat people. He knew that we would look after his boat, and bring it back nice and clean and tidy. If you could see some of the hire boats when they come back in, they are like a tip. He used to say 'if all our boats come in like yours, I wouldn't want any cleaners'.

I must be one of the oldest boatmen still on the canals. I know I stopped carrying some years ago, but I have never left the canal. I have always had a boat of some description, and I still have half share in a historic boat. I go to about six boat rallies every year. I don't know how long I can keep going, as I am 82 years old. I don't feel my age. I am lucky as my father died age 46 in 1949, but my father had a hard life with horse boats, until he had motor boat.

Recent Events

by Mavis Blunn, July 2016

John and Mary, and Jack and I had moved to Wheaton Aston in 1969 within months of each other. With John working for British Waterways at the lock, we soon became friends, and John and Mary sometimes babysat Lucy.

Lucy married Nick in 1998, and moved to Hereford. John retired, and he and Mary went off boating, so we lost touch. Life was to change dramatically for Lucy, Nick, Jack and I. We got a derelict 30ft boat, and that was all the boating that Jack and I did. Jack went into hospital for a hip replacement and Lucy sold the boat in July 2003.

Lucy later bought Jack a Father's Day present, a 1930s 70ft Grand Union small Woolwich boat, *Cepheus*. Unfortunately, Jack had a stroke in hospital, and died as a result, so although he knew about the boat, he never saw it.

Jack had always said as a joke, perhaps, that he would want a boatman's funeral, so we went to see the funeral director in Penkridge, and he was wonderful. We painted *Cepheus* up with help from friends, and were able to take Jack from the wharf at Wheaton Aston to the bridge above the lock, then by road to the church at Lapley for interment. It was amazing. Roger Hipkiss steered *Cepheus*, and Dilwyn Griffiths did the lock. About 30 friends followed on the towpath. Afterwards, we had a great party at the village hall; everyone brought food, and it was a real goodbye.

Mary, John's wife, died on 2 December 2004 from a brain tumour, and Lucy and I went to her funeral. I hadn't seen John since he had retired. Lucy was moving to New Zealand, and asked John to look after *Cepheus* as I couldn't cope with her. That was great for both of us – it gave us a sense of purpose in life. John and I took *Cepheus* to quite a few boat rallies, and John enjoyed a chance to get back on the cut.

Unfortunately, in 2008, Lucy had to sell *Cepheus*, as living in New Zealand made it difficult, though it broke her heart. In June 2008, Lucy, John and I took the former Fellows, Morton & Clayton motor boat *Cactus* to Middlewich for Malcom Braine – a great trip.

Lucy's life changed after her divorce, and as well as running her company in New Zealand, she took a short term work contract in the UK to bolster her finances. As money was short for a house, a boat was the obvious answer. In 2010, she looked at a few, and while we were in Braunston, a good friend of John's told us that John Saxon was selling *Lion*. I had had *Lion* in 1961 at Aylesbury, when she was 45ft long, but had sold her to move to Wheaton Aston. John Saxon had bought her and had her lengthened with two sections, 10ft and 15ft, to restore her to full length. The sale was all settled within a month. John Saxon was glad that *Lion* was coming home again. As John had used her as a holiday boat, and Lucy wanted her as a liveaboard, she was completely gutted. The solid fuel fire was removed, and a diesel fire and radiators were fitted. Bunks were removed, and a new wooden floor was laid at Norbury Junction while the boat was frozen in there at Christmas. John refitted all the interior to suit Lucy's needs. In 2012, we had the boat out of the water at Stretton for an insurance survey. We found to our horror that we needed 20ft of new bottoms. The cheap Japanese steel had worn down to 2mm. We also decided to change the engine as it was a water cooled Fowler diesel, which was great for a 45ft boat, but not really enough power now for a 70ft boat. Lucy bought a Lister HR2 air cooled engine – much better. We changed *Lion's* name back to the original 1925 name, *The North*.

John and I were getting older, so in 2012, John sold his Park home in Penkridge, and moved in with me in Wheaton Aston; it made sense at that time. John bought half of *The North* from Lucy – she was now a family boat again. Lucy was now full time back in New Zealand, after her contract ended in the UK, as life over there would be much better for her. John and I continued to go to the rallies, and enjoy life on the cut. Lucy came over when she could, and we had some great trips, while John and I visited New Zealand several times to see how Lucy was getting on over there.

Some interior work, new batteries, and the installation of a third 2-berth cabin made *The North* virtually finished by August 2015. John and I decided to take the plunge and get married, in a very simple ceremony with just two witnesses – my friend Heather, and Ray Butler off *Owl*. This was followed by a wonderful party on 5 September 2015.

John and I went to visit Lucy in January 2016, and we all decided that *The North*, much as all love her, is now too large for us. Built as a liveaboard, she usually had just John and I, and sometimes Lucy, on board. So we all decided to put her up for sale, though we are in no hurry. We will only be using her for rallies.

At the moment, we have just left the event in Lymm on the Bridgewater Canal in June, and will go to several more rallies this year. If *The North* does sell, then John and I will look for something around 45ft to 50ft, just for holidays – but who knows when that will happen?

But we will never leave the cut!

Also published or distributed by Canal Book Shop - www.canalbookshop.co.uk

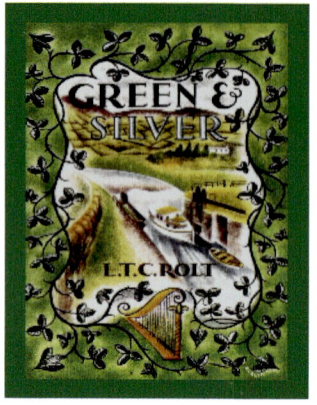

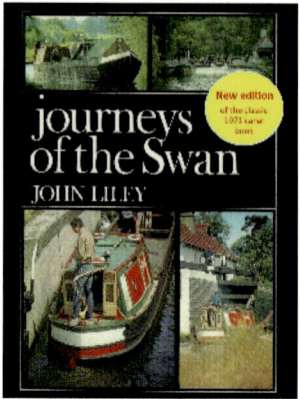

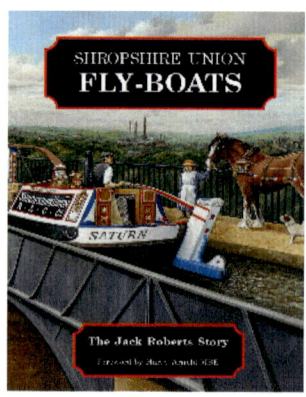

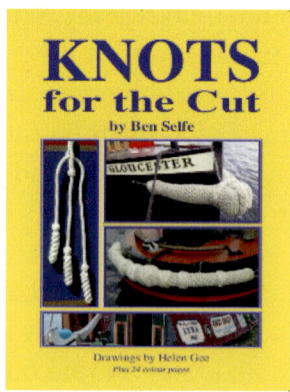

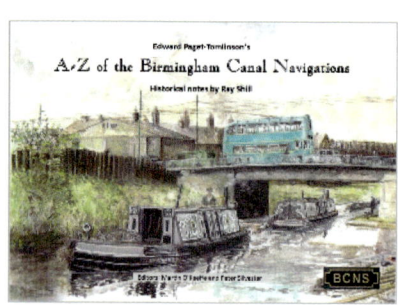